I0022437

Anonymus

Our Established Church

Anonymus

Our Established Church

ISBN/EAN: 9783742812223

Manufactured in Europe, USA, Canada, Australia, Japa

Cover: Foto ©Thomas Meinert / pixelio.de

Manufactured and distributed by brebook publishing software
(www.brebook.com)

Anonymus

Our Established Church

"Our Established Church:"

THE NOTORIOUS ARTICLE IN PUTNAM'S MAGAZINE, JULY, 1869.

TOGETHER WITH THE ARTICLE

"THE UNESTABLISHED CHURCH,"

(PUTNAM'S MAGAZINE, DECEMBER, 1869,)

IN WHICH IT IS

TRIUMPHANTLY REFUTED!

WITH AN EXPLANATORY AND EXCULPATORY PREFACE, AND SUNDRY

NOTICES OF THE CONTEMPORARY PRESS.

———

NEW YORK:
G. P. PUTNAM & SON, 4TH AVENUE AND 23D STREET.
1870.

NOTICES OF THE PRESS.

"Startling at first * * * fully justified by the array of facts which it presents." "Who can find fault with the writer who, using plain terms, calls this 'Our Established Church?'"—*New York Evangelist.*

"May well make the reader grave who reads it with his mind as well as with his eyes. It is admirably written, with a dignity that is not injured by the satire that pervades it * * * ."—*New York Tribune.*

"Too malicious for pleasantry, and too untrue for wit. * * * Sensational writer. * * * Attempts to be so ironical and so witty, and so readily sacrifices sobriety and truth to point. * * * Has disgusted all fair-minded and moderate Protestants."—*Catholic World.*

"Full of serious facts, thoughtfully and powerfully presented."—*New York Evening Post.*

"A new crusade against Catholicism."—*New York Herald.*

"—— which we trust every American will read."—*New York Evening Press.*

"I do not wish to review the article in *Putnam*, but claim the privilege of correcting some of its misstatements."—*Right Rev. B. J. McQuaid, D.D., Bishop of Rochester.*

"What do you propose to do about it?"—*Idem.*

"A remarkable article."—*Cleveland Leader.*

"The author's zeal * * * had got the better of his judgment. Some of his errors were obvious; * * * but others, not so apparent, Bishop McQuaid, of Western New York, points out. * * * The bishop is in a position to know whereof he speaks."—*New York Times.*

"Some boldly denounce the writer as a concealed enemy of religious liberty, and an insidious friend of the Roman Catholic Church as a State Church."—*New York Christian Advocate.*

"Most striking article * * * an anonymous attack * * * . The essay is too ironical; perhaps it would be so, being ironical at all. To serve efficiently any cause which depends for success on the support of a majority of the legal voters, on its getting for adherents twenty-six electors out of every 'forty-nine fools and one wise man' in all the precincts, the popular orators and advocates cannot be too careful to shun the fine-drawn and the subtle, and trust to plain and direct statements and hard hammering of argument. The clever writer in *Putnam's* certainly succeeds, however, in making an impressive case."—*The Nation.*

"We venture to predict a wide notoriety."—*Independent.*

"Its keen, withering irony, * * * the deep significance of its facts."—*Cleveland Herald.*

"Unworthy of notice." "It was a waste of time for Bishop McQuaid to have answered the article." * * * "A feeble effort."—*New York Leader.*

"The incendiarism of the writer and his partisans does not lack for assurance. * * * This writer and his friends, who can so coolly put forth statements and observations that outrage the best moral sense of the present age. * * * This man may scoff at the impersonal 'people;' he may gravely advise to give up celebrating Washington's birthday as 'cold and perfunctory,' and substitute St. Patrick's instead, but he had better wait till he sees it done."— *Lynn (Mass.) Transcript.*

" Perhaps the most important paper, political or social, which has appeared in the last ten years."—*American Churchman, Chicago and Milwaukee.*

" A brilliant article." * * * " Caught publishing apocryphal statements in regard to the Romish Church."—*American Presbyterian.*

" If we do not exceedingly mistake, almost any candid reader will see at once that it is an honest and genuine Catholic paper. For ourselves, we have no question about it. But its barefaced and demanding tone have rather overshot the mark, it would seem ; and Catholics now, disturbed at the premature audacity of their able brother, turn and deny that he is a Catholic at all ; declaring that, instead, the article is the feigned work of some designing Protestant ! No wonder ! "—*Lynn Transcript* (a second article).

" I have learned that the author of the article in *Putnam's Magazine* is a Protestant, and his name is Parsons."—*The Rev. Patrick Strain, Pastor of St. Mary's Church, Lynn,* in his public controversy with the *Transcript.*

[The publishers of *Putnam* desire to suggest this conjectural theory of the origin of the statement just quoted. It is related that a wayfaring countryman of the Rev. Mr. Strain, reposing himself at midday at the side of the highway, observed on the opposite side of the road a plain hewn stone, with a simple inscription :

90

MILES

From Boston.

" Poor old man," ejaculated the traveller. " So they buried him right here, by the roadside ! And he was ninety years old, and his name was Miles, from Boston ! " We apprehend that, out of the statement by some ill-informed and possibly malicious person, the author of our article, whatever his name, was " a Protestant Parson," the very natural error of the pastor of St. Mary's arose.]

" Some one has contributed [to the December *Putnam*] an ironical review of ' Our Established Church,' but it is hard to tell sometimes which side the writer is writing on."—*New York Observer.*

" More satisfactory " [than the July article]. " More cogent in its statement of the case : * * * exposes very well the disingenuousness of the *Catholic World.*"—*The Nation.*

" Decidedly, not to say maliciously, wrong." * * * " Regarding the unsupported statement of the writer as presumptive evidence of falsehood rather than of truth, we let the charge pass." " The writer attempts to be witty, but succeeds only in being abusive. Wit does not appear to be his strong point, and his attempts at it only provoke a smile at his expense."—*Catholic World, January,* 1870.

PREFACE.

Vox emissa volat! The injurious speech, once set afloat upon the breeze, is not easily recalled or limited in its career. Denial or refutation, too, toils after it almost in vain. And if the calumny, or the ill-advised eulogy which is sometimes more damaging than calumny, has happened to set in motion the tongues of many men, refutation and denial may quite as well abide at home and hold their peace.

Hopeless, therefore, of counteracting by silence the effect of an article published last July, under the title, " Our Established Church," which has achieved an unusual notoriety, the publishers of *Putnam's Magazine* make this concession to the demand which has been made for a new edition. But that with the obnoxious thing, wherever it goes, may go also the antidote, and to vindicate also their own justice and fairness, the publishers send with it into the world the searching review and sharp correction served out to it in their *Magazine* for December last.

To the completeness of this confutation it should seem to be unnecessary to add a word. But the same periodical (called the *The Catholic World*), which was among the earliest and most eager in denouncing the " Established Church " paper, strangely enough assails, if possible with greater vehemence, the paper which controverts the former, and treats the same Church as " Unestablished." It is hardly likely that, if we should give up another dozen papers of *Putnam* to a surrejoinder to this latest pleading of the *World*, we should get the case at last into a form entirely satisfactory to our somewhat shrewish contemporary. But it is surely no more than fair that we should utter a closing protest against certain misapprehensions of fact, and certain misconceptions of the sentiments and purposes of ourselves, of the author of our first paper, and of the author of our second, which are indicated in the article, " Putnam's Defence," in *The Catholic World* for January.

We shall be permitted, then, in the first place, to declare positively and solemnly that, while we know, far better than the " Catholic Publication Society " can know, who the authors of the peccant articles of July and December are, we are also as well convinced of their motives and feelings regarding the matters they discuss as we are of our own. The open and palpable contradiction of their opinions, expressed as it is in the very titles of their papers, we do not pretend to reconcile. But we do undertake to assert, with the confidence of an intimate knowledge, that however those writers may differ in their views of the position held by the Roman Catholic Church in this State, it is a baseless assumption or wilful detraction to attribute to either of them the malevolence which it is the main criticism of *The Catholic World* to impute. We deny and denounce, with as much emphasis as the reverence due the clerical order will admit, the charge that either article is " written in an unsuccessful vein of irony," or is " directed against the honor " of the Church ; that either writer " attempts to be witty, but succeeds only in being abusive," or "hates" the Church "with a hatred equal to that of the wicked Jews for our Lord whom they crucified between two thieves;" while candor compels us to admit that both, while approving the liberation of the Church, would yet insist on the crucifixion of the thieves. We further concede, promptly and frankly, and with some sense of humiliation, that it should be deemed a concession that "wit is not the strong point" of either. And although we cannot agree with *The Catholic World* that their "strong point is hatred of the Church," we might be at a loss if required to say exactly what it was. Perhaps we should say, a painstaking but plodding investigation of facts, which they do not succeed in agreeing how to explain : perhaps, in the case of the former, a somewhat extravagant and unregulated ecclesiasticism ; in the case of the latter, we might suggest, a new and over-liberal, though rare, type of American Gallicanism.

When we have vouched our July number, as reprinted herewith, to witness that it did not "*condemn* the Church as Our Established Church," but, on the contrary, commended and applauded it ; and our December number to witness that it did not "condemn it as the Unestablished Church," but applauded and glorified it on the contrary, we have said perhaps enough in vindication of the sentiments of our contributors, at least against attacks from the Catholic side. To the violent and "railing accusations" that have been brought against them from the opposite quarter, we have, at present, no response to make. Assaults of that kind, from such sources, our writers were bound to expect and to be prepared for. Their work could not be a pleasant one to Protestants ; and we are justified in saying that the measure of favor, amounting sometimes almost to approbation, which these productions have met with among Protestants, has astonished no one so much as the writers themselves.

So much by way of repelling unfounded accusations against our contributors in regard to their sentiments and motives. Before we go on to reasseverate, even to iteration, their actual belief and expectation as to the future of the Roman Catholic Church in this country, we are bound to dispose of an issue or two of fact in the latest article in the *World*. Our July article contained the statement that the State of New York, in 1866, out of $129,025.14 paid to benefactions under religious control, gave $124,174.14 to our friends the Catholics. *The Catholic World* denied this ; that is, it alleged that it had no knowledge or information thereof sufficient to form a belief. Our December article reaffirmed the statement, and referred to the report of the State Comptroller for 1866, at pages 71 to 75, quoting therefrom the several items which made up the two totals, with the addition to each of one sum of $1,000, which had been overlooked before. *The Catholic World* now "has the Comptroller's report before it ; has examined and reëxamined it, and does not find the statement in it, or any thing to warrant it."

This attack, we confess, staggers us. We can think of but two ways to meet it : (1.) We have had the Comptroller's report before us ; have examined and reëxamined it, and find the precise words and figures in it already given ; and beg leave again to refer to it, *loc. cit.* (2.) When it was reported to Admiral Nelson, in the midst of the battle of Copenhagen, that his commander-in-chief was flying the signal to retire from action, that distinguished officer applied his glass to his blind eye, "examined and reëxamined" the mast-head of his superior's ship, and deliberately concluded that he did not find such a signal there, nor any thing that looked like it.*

---

* This "little story" is open to criticism on two grounds : it is not new, and it is not wholly to the point against *The Catholic World*, because Lord Nelson's remark was really true.

We ought to add a word upon the same general subject. Our Paulist brethren, who carry to such a degree the Pauline injunction, to be all things to all men, that they must, in the course of events, become horribly uncivil to somebody, observe that the statement quoted from the Comptroller's report " has been more than once pronounced on the highest authority and proved to be a forgery, as the *Magazine* well knows, or is inexcusable for not knowing." This is a very shocking accusation. The country is already too familiar with bare unsupported charges against high public officers ; but is it possible that the Comptroller of this State can falsify his accounts in this audacious and shameless manner, to the value of a hundred thousand dollars, with no further penalty than an excoriation from *The Catholic World?* There are his figures : were these moneys, then, never paid ? The Treasurer's report, too, agrees with the Comptroller's ; was the Treasurer, then, a confederate ? It is true, the matter has not been suffered to pass altogether *sub silentio.* " The Hon. Mr. Cassidy " (apparently of Greek descent, and probably of Buddhist faith), " of the Albany *Atlas and Argus,* declared [the statement] false from beginning to end.* The Hon. Mr. Alvord, the distinguished member from Onondaga county, did the same." Just *here,* we think, should come in the *World's* ejaculation : " For honest and fair-minded men *this* was conclusive." And we may well leave out the authority of Mr. Roberts, of the *Utica Herald,* which unquestionably is weighty, to whichever side it leans. Our interest in Mr. Roberts' opinion was deep enough to move us to inquire of him what his utterances upon this subject really had been ; and we learn, somewhat to our relief, that he has not found fault with the Comptroller's report, and that he has pronounced neither that nor our statistics " a forgery." This accusation, in fact, as applied to statistics, we suspect is new with the *World.* We have heard of " false " statistics before, as we have heard, for example, of " forged " Decretals. But when it is so easy to falsify figures, it is a mere wantonness of crime to resort to forgery when the poorest original invention would serve the purpose. And the able and dignified leader, which Mr. Roberts sends us as the only thing he has published which could give color to the invocation of his authority by the *World,* calls nothing whatever a " forgery," but criticises certain statements, of which it is enough to say that they are not our statements. To the Comptroller's report, then, so long as that official for 1866 keeps out of State's Prison, we still appeal ; though, if the *World* shall continue to threaten us with that severer punishment hinted at in calling upon " our friend, the Rev. Leonard W. Bacon, who sometimes writes for *Putnam,*" and who is a scourge of evil-doers, we may be terrified into silence.

We proceed, now, to the final clearing up, we hope, of a subject of contention in regard to which the general public appears to be exceedingly uninformed, and which has only been plunged in deeper confusion by the attempts of our warring contributors and of their hostile critics to throw light upon it. The writer in July, after recounting several benefactions in the way of land-grants from the municipal government of New York to the Church he was pleased to speak of as " Established," proceeded : " Upon some part of this property, or upon another tract held by a like title and upon similar terms, is in course of erection the new St. Patrick's Cathedral," &c. A foot-note to this passage essays a bit of satire (although this writer is singularly destitute of any ordinary sense of humor) upon an eminent ethical writer, Mr. Parton, who, in the *Atlantic* for April, 1868, had extolled " the foresight of Archbishop Hughes in buying this tract at a time when

---

* It is to be regretted that no effort has been made to preserve a record of the views upon this subject of the Hon. Terence McManis, Member of Assembly from the Sixth Ward of New York. It is hardly doubtful, however, that they coincided, as they usually did, with those of the Hon. Mr. Cassidy.

other purchasers would not;" and suggests that "a willingness to risk one dollar a year for a block of lots on Fifth Avenue, any time within fifteen years, could hardly have been deemed a wild passion for speculation." In this indiscreet limitation of time to the past "fifteen years" was presented the happy opportunity of that vigorous controversialist, the Bishop of Rochester. When that venerable prelate shied his hat into the arena, it was just here that he planted his first and most effective blow. "The new St. Patrick's Cathedral" (writes Bishop McQuaid to the newspapers) "stands on ground purchased by Catholics about sixty years ago, and ever since in their possession. This fact spoils Parton's compliment to the late Archbishop Hughes' foresight, and a nice bit of irony in *Putnam's Magazine.*" *The Catholic World*, in August, repeated the bishop's correction with emphasis; and the writer of "*The Unestablished Church*" enumerated the error thus pointed out as one of the two ascertained errors in the earlier article. We are able, now, to add, for the vindication of the bishop and the confusion of his adversaries, the fact that the block on which the cathedral is rising, bounded by 50th and 51st-streets and 4th and 5th Avenues, was formerly known as Block No. 62 of the Common Lands, owned by the Mayor, Aldermen, and Commonalty of the city of New York. That, on the 1st of May, 1799 (more than the bishop's "sixty years ago"), this plot was *leased* (not sold) by the city, for the annual rent of four bushels of wheat. But inasmuch as a lease, even at so moderate a rental, was not thought convenient for building purposes, it was very simply converted into a fee by a release, on the 11th of November, 1852, from the Mayor, Aldermen, and Commonalty of New York to "The Trustees of St. Patrick's Cathedral, and James R. Bailey and James B. Nicholson, new Trustees," &c., of the city's fee in the premises, for the very considerable sum of $83.32. All these things—and how many more of the same kind it would take an infinite amount of labor to discover —are they not written in the Record-Books of the Register's Office in the City Hall Park? We venture to say that, if the author of "*Our Established Church*" had known exactly what they were and where to find them, there would have been less occasion given for contradiction to his loose and unverified guesses.

It must have been from a consciousness of having driven a hard bargain with the "Trustees" in extorting this $83.32, that when the city government extended Madison avenue across this block in 1864 (not greatly to the detriment of the property), it contributed no less than $24,000 in payment for the strip of land necessary to be taken. If any one has difficulty in comprehending the economy of this way of doing business, we can only give the familiar explanation of the Chatham-street merchant, to whom the rustic expressed surprise that he could make money by selling always "below cost." "I couldn't, my friend, if I didn't do *so much of it.*"

Before going further, we must do our *Magazine* an act of justice to its consistency. Our *Catholic* neighbor errs in saying that it "withdraws its false statement as to the millions of property held in fee-simple by the five bishops in the State." Its statement in July was, that the millions of property were owned, in great part, "by one or another of five ecclesiastics." Under correction of the Bishop of Rochester, it admitted, in December, that that dignitary had not received his share, which was owned by Bishop Loughlin, of Brooklyn. And inasmuch as the original statement would have remained unshaken if the Bishops of Albany and Buffalo had also complained that the Brooklyn ecclesiastic had their shares as well, since the property would still have been held "by one or another of five ecclesiastics," we have not thought, and really cannot think, of "withdrawing" a statement so absolutely correct. At the same time, we must admit that there is much force in the argument urged by the *World* in regard to the Catholic Religious Society Law of 1863, that it only secures to " *the Church* the free manage-ment of her own temporalities." This is, indeed, exactly what that law effectually does ; and it is what is done for no other than *the* Church by the laws of this State, or, so far as we are advised, of any American common-wealth. To no point heretofore has the legislation of New York at least been more sedulously directed than to the absolute removal from the churches of the control of the temporalities devoted to their use, and the maintenance in every case of religious societies separate from and independ-ent of the churches, and sometimes, as it has happened, antagonistic to them, and subversive to their faith and order. We do not propose to vindicate this system of legislation ; very likely it may be quite the thing for the sects of dissent ; we merely recall the unquestionable fact, illustrated as it is every year by instances of the property given and held for the religious uses of one sect, being turned over to those of another by the action of a society foreign to the church, and made up of whatever members of another church, or of no church, or of a Tom Paine Club, may have attended worship there for a year, and contributed to the expenses of the society. But does *The Catholic World* really believe that the Act of 1863, in giving such control to the Church, " only secures to it equal rights with the sects ? " Does it fancy that the Protestant Episcopal Church, which is, no less than the Roman Catholic, a general organization extending throughout and far beyond the limits of the State, and, no less than that, assumes to be a great spiritual unit, " controls the temporalities " devoted to Episcopalian worship ? Does it imagine to itself the Right Rev. Bishop Potter enforcing his pastoral authority over St. George's, in New York, by closing its doors upon the flock which his shepherd's crook has first expelled into the street ? Or can it frame the picture even of a Diocesan Convention, or of a General Conven-tion—bodies of a higher legislative and administrative authority in that Church than any known in the Roman Church this side of Rome—attempt-ing a like " control of temporalities " in regard to St. George's, or even essaying to extinguish a candle at the altar of little St. Alban's ? Can it conceive of any case in any non-Catholic sect where the spiritual body, call-ing itself the Church, or the governing powers of it, however constituted, can exercise the slightest legal authority over the property it uses ? We think not. We *know* it cannot. And just here is the difference. Just here is the power the State grants the Roman Church, which it withholds from every other Church. We thank it for withholding ; we do not complain of it for granting ; only, we congratulate the Church.

If to any reader the distinction between the spiritual body, the Church, and the body corporate, the society, be so subtle as to evade him, or seem so slight that he can see no importance in restricting the powers of either, let him imagine the authorities of the former body, of whatever name, whether its governing power be vested in a majority of communicants, or in a ses-sion, or a convocation, or an uncontrolled chief or bishop, to seek to impose some new dogma or oppressive discipline upon unwilling parishioners, whose money, and their fathers' money, has provided the land and buildings applied to pious uses. Before the Act of 1863, in all churches—and now in all churches but the Roman—the means of enforcing the spiritual decree are spiritual means—argument, appeal, admonition. If these fail, the Church yields, or, at worst, cuts off the disobedient, to worship God in their own way in the house their means have procured them. Under the Act of 1863, the subjects yield ; the simple alternative to implicit obedience and submis-sion is not merely the spiritual penalties so heavy in any ecclesiastical hands, but the expulsion from all that they had paid for, built, and fancied that they

owned.   What if the Catholic laity of New York were to a man hostile (as
we have not the least reason to suppose they are) to the dogma of infallibility?   Suppose even that the Vatican Council should refuse to decree it.
Suppose, then, that it should be announced, nevertheless, from the See of St.
Peter, under the usual damnatory clauses, as essential to salvation.   No one
doubts where the five bishops of New York would be.   No one has any
right to doubt that the fifty millions of church property in this State would
be as absolutely and irretrievably, and as utterly without control from the
million or two of Catholic laymen who have helped pay for it, at the disposal
of an Italian prince, as the poorest rural Baptist chapel is under the power
of its unanimous congregation.   We may even suppose a stronger case.   We
are at liberty to imagine the event that the voluntary contributions of the
faithful should no longer suffice, as heretofore, to maintain the disciplined
legions who protect the throne of the Sovereign Pontiff more successfully
against domestic dissent than against foreign aggression, and who are capable
of considerable severity when not too formidably opposed—*Zouaviter in
modo*, as well as *fortiter in re*—as appeared from the sack of Perugia in 1859.
No more effectual way could be devised for a sudden emergency of reinforcing
the Peter's pence than to levy upon the church property of fifty millions in
this State a contribution of say ten per cent., to be raised by mortgages.
Our five bishops—or four, if they prefer—object (we mean to make the case
a strong one).   By the speedy communication of the mails, or even the
quicker operation of the telegraph, a prompt and sweeping process of translation occurs.   Our venerated archbishop finds himself promoted in a twink-
ling to the arch-diocese of New Archangel; and the present right reverend
bishops of Brooklyn, Albany, Rochester, and Buffalo are all given truly
apostolic work at the sees of El Medina, Timbuctoo, Terra del Fuego, and
Tananarivo, all *in partibus*, and five more submissive ecclesiastics from the
College of the Propaganda, if they could not be found nearer, are installed
in their places.   By the instant operation of the Act of 1863, each one of
these five became instantly a member of every religious society in his diocese, organized under it.   Of course, he appoints a vicar-general to suit him;
and if any parish priest is not fully to his mind, he replaces such by others
entirely satisfactory; and the new vicar-general and the new priests, becoming at once, by force of the Act, members of the religious societies in place
of the old, it remains to arrange about two laymen who, with the other and
satisfactory three, constitute the entire board.   It is enough to say, that the
dissent of such a minority could be of little avail; but if the moral effect of
unanimity be desired, the clerical three have only to wait until the corporate
year comes round, and to fill their places, as the Act provides, with two of
whose subservience there can be no question.   Then let them execute their
mortgage, and remit the proceeds in gold or drafts, as the instructions from
Rome require.   Is it not simple?   And if any one objects, what of it?

     Exactly this fact it was upon which our July writer, in part, depended to
justify him in calling the Roman Church "Established;" the fact that the
Roman Church alone, among churches, had been favored by the State by
entrusting to it—to the spiritual body and the spiritual hierarchy—the absolute control of its enormous endowments.   And upon just this fact, too, did
the December writer, in part, rest in rebuking the former for his epithet,
since in no other land in Christendom has an established hierarchy the like
tremendous power.   If compelled to arbitrate between them, we could hardly
say but both were right.

     We have been saying a good deal thus far—perhaps too much—in excul-
pation of ourselves and our contributors.   We are bound to add, before
sending the following papers again into the world, something in mere justice

to the *World*, whose reputation for orthodoxy might suffer at Rome if the accusations of our *Magazine* should reach there unaccompanied by the explanations and excuses put forth in January. It is an act of judicial impartiality, which we willingly perform, to give them full currency herewith.

" We are accused, because we say the Church here desires no establishment by law—*for she has what is better than such establishment*—of contradicting the *Syllabus*, and *going against* [*sic*] the supreme pontiff. *We accept the Syllabus without the slightest reserve*, though probably not in the *Magazine's* sense."

[This is doing very well, so far. We know, now, pretty well, where to find the " liberal Catholics " of this country. The hint in the last six words does not in the least becloud the matter. If our good friends will stand to *any* sense the monkish Latin of that document can be twisted into, they will give us the special satisfaction of knowing where they are.
We confess, at the same time, to some curiosity to know in what sense— whether " the sense of the *Syllabus*," or other—one Father Hecker, whose name appears on the cover of *The Catholic World*, declared in a public lecture, a year or two since, as reported in the newspapers, that " there is, ere long, to be a State religion in this country, and that State religion is to be Roman Catholic." Can the *World* explain ?]

" The *Syllabus* condemns those who demand the separation of Church and State *in the sense of the European liberals ;* but not us for not requiring the Church to be established by law as the State-Church."

[We do not find the italicised words of limitation in the Syllabus. We fancied, indeed, that that instrument had an Ecumenical character, and was as keen for the dividing asunder of joints and marrow of Massachusetts or Ohio schismatics, of Nestorian or Coptic heretics, as of " European liberals." But as too great publicity cannot be given to a good thing, we repeat here, in juxtaposition with the last extract, Damnable Errors Nos. 55 and 77.

55. That the Church must be separated from the State, and the State from the Church.
77. That in the present day it is no longer necessary that the Catholic religion shall be held as *the only religion of the State, to the exclusion* of all other modes of worship.]

Those liberals mean, by the separation of Church and State, *the independence of the State*, and its right to pursue its own policy, irrespective of the rights and interests of religion. *In that sense* [not merely, therefore, it will be seen, in a " parliamentary " or " Pickwickian " sense] we also condemn the separation, and are continually warring against it as political atheism. But *we deny that* in that sense, or in the sense of the *Syllabus, we do or ever have advocated the separation of Church and State.*   *   *   *   An Act of the Legislature of the State or the nation forbidding Christianity, or authorizing acts directly against it, would be null and void from the beginning, and be treated by the courts as would be a *jus municipium* [*sic*] in violation of the *jus gentium.*

We trust the readers of this pamphlet will not think us over-exact in seeking to interpret the utterances of *The Catholic World*. In all earnestness, we deem it difficult to exaggerate their importance. They come from a class of writers whose fault has never been, these many centuries, a loose and generous frankness ; they touch upon matters of the last importance, not merely in a religious view—for, upon that, *Putnam's Magazine* has been always careful not to touch in the slightest—but in a purely political aspect, as they might appear to one who looked upon all creeds as alike false ; they are the forced expressions under the stress of public inquisition, and guarded by the keenest caution of a tremendous power which hopes shortly to be ready to act. Nor is the weight of this particular sentence impaired by the

somewhat nebulous illustration at its close. Our clerical friends may write
bad Latin, if they choose ; no sacerdotal prerogative is more firmly established by the usage of centuries than that; and the less Latin the reader
knows, the more likely he is to understand what Cicero, though a Roman and
a lawyer, would never have guessed, that "*jus municipium*" is used to mean
"municipal law." It is plain that the writer fancies that an American court,
if a State or Federal statute appears to contravene a principle of interna-
tional law, would hold it "null and void." We imagine that this principle
of jurisprudence will startle the jurisconsult as much as the Latin phrase
alarms the linguist. But what is of far higher importance, what rises above
all trifling criticism, is the fact that here we have an authoritative announcement, partial though it be, of the principle that shall guide our future Catholic rulers. The people governed must await with profound anxiety the
decisions of that Catholic judiciary which is to say what the " Christianity "
is which legislation is not to contravene. We surmise that it will fare hard
with sectaries then.

We have left ourselves but little space—though more, perhaps, than we
need—to comment upon the latest observations of *The Catholic World* in
regard to the common school system. We had already observed, with some
regret, that our December writer had expressed somewhat earnestly a feeling
which is not so much a Protestant, or religious, as an American, or political
and social feeling, that our system of public education is a good thing, and a
thing to be maintained at any price. The existence and the earnestness of
this sentiment is not to be denied ; but if the writer in December thinks it
useful to give expression to it, we are bound to differ with him. So far as
the State of New York is concerned, the system of public education is dead.
A system of sectarian education, sustained at public expense, but superior to
public interference, is established in its place ; a system which received last
year, in the city of New York alone, $215,000 from a single fund (an annual
gift made perpetual by the statute authorizing it), besides large and numerous
subsidies from other public sources, and the strongest argument for the per-
manence of which is found in the fact that one quarter of the sum mentioned
was accepted by non-Catholic schools.*

* The details of these subventions in the city of New York in 1869, so far as we have been able to
ascertain them, we submit below. Our experience with the data extracted from the State Comptroller's
report compels us to anticipate severe treatment for any thing we may offer in the way of figures. We
hasten, therefore, to admit that these statistics are imperfect, and that whenever we can learn of additional donations to like purposes, we shall be happy to correct our tables by inserting them.

TABLE OF MONEYS VOTED FROM THE PUBLIC TREASURY OF THE CITY OF NEW YORK FOR
SECTARIAN INSTITUTIONS IN 1869.

ROMAN CATHOLIC..$112,062.26

Sacred Heart Convent $10,000	St. Joseph's Parish School $2,000
Sacred Heart School.......................... 4,000	St. Joseph's Male School.................. 3,180
House Good Shepherd........................ 25,000	St. Joseph's Female School................ 3,410
House Good Shepherd........................ 15,000	St. Teresa's School........................ 7,730
House Mercy................................ 6,000	St. Teresa's Church....................... 640
Sisters Mercy................................ 457	School St. Teresa's Chapel................. 6,000
Sisters St. Dominic.......................... 10,000	St. Teresa's School........................ 5,100
Sisters St. Dominic.......................... 106	St. Ann's School........................... 1,600
Asylum St. Dominic.......................... 5,000	St. Ann's Church........................... 208
Dominican Fathers 2,774	St. Peter's School.......................... 6,000
Dominican Church........................... 3,500	Ger. Am. St. Peter's School................ 1,600
St. Nicholas School...................·····.. 6,800	Ger. Am. Free School...................... 14,000
St. Nicholas School.......................... 6,000	St. Lawrence Church....................... 1,600
St. Nicholas Church.......................... 364	St. Lawrence Parish School................ 6,000
St. Patrick's Orphan Asylum 8,153	St. Mary's School 20,000
St. Patrick's Cathedral...................... 8,928	St. Mary's Church.......................... 200
St. Patrick's School 8,000	Sisters of Charity 70
St. Patrick's Orphan Asylum................ 5,000	Most Holy Redeemer School................ 11,000
St. Bridget's School 23,540	St. Francis Female School.................. 4,250
St. Bridget's Church......................... 6,800	St. Francis Male School 3,750
Sister Helena.............................. 4,317	St. Francis Hospital........................ 6,000
Sisters of St. Joseph........................ 5,000	St. Michael's School........................ 2,500
St. Joseph's Church.......................... 2,071	St. Michael's School........................ 6,000
St. Joseph's Orphan Asylum................. 5,000	St. Michael's School........................ 5,000

PREFACE. xiii

We know that public schools, established under the ancient system, continue to exist; that under some name and for some purposes—"pauper-

St. Gabriel's School	$11,830	St. John's School for Girls	$2,140
Church of Transfiguration	387	Church of Nativity School	639
Transfiguration School	11,500	R. C. Church	645
St. James' Male School	6,000	Holy Cross Church	2,123
St. James' Female School	7,000	Holy Cross Church School	1,272
St. James' Church	800	St. Matthew's Church	463
Our Lady of Sorrow School	8,000	Church of the Assumption	459
St. Columbia School	6,120	Church St. John the Baptist	533
Holy Innocents' School	562	St. Vincent's Hospital	10,000
St. Andrew's Church	1,007	St. Vincent's R. C. Orphan Asylum	15,000
Church of the Immaculate Conception	5,000	St. Stephen's Orphan House	5,000
School of the Immaculate Conception	10,000	St. Stephen's Orphan House	3,000
Church of St. Paul	5,004	R. Burtsell, to taxes 22d-st. Church property	505
St. Vincent de Paul School	2,540	German School	5,000
German American School	3,150	German Mission Association	5,000
St. Boniface Church	965		

PROTESTANT EPISCOPAL..$29,335.09

St. Bartholomew's Church	$263	N. Y. Prot. Epis. Missionary Society	$600
St. Luke's Hospital	842	St. John's Chapel School	975
St. Lukes Hospital for Indigent Females	5,000	Shepherd's Fold	500
St. Luke's Hospital Parochial School	271	Holy Apostles' Church	179
Incarnation Church	2,810	Sepulchre Church	750
St. Philip's P. K. Church	290	St. Clement's Prot. Epis. Church	156
St. Phillip's Church	159	St. Mark's Church	689
St. Paul's Chapel School	758	All Angels' Church	1,177
Holy Trinity Church	1,270	All Saints' Church	529
Trinity Church School	704	Church of Intercession	1,749
Trinity Chapel School	650	St. Mary's Episcopal Church	323
St. Timothy's Church	1,785	St. Mary's Episcopal Church, Sisterhood	3,000
St. Mary's Church	257	Zion Church	69
School Church Redeemer	1,000	Sheltering Arms School	1,000
N. Y. Prot. Epis. Church	1,200	Memorial Church	370

HEBREW..$14,404.49

Cong. Shearith Israel	$940	Cong. B. Israel	$68
Cong. Anslie Chesed	402	Cong. Adircth El	191
Hebrew School, No. 1	2,280	Hebrew Benevolent Society Orphan Asylum	5,000
Polonies Talmud K. School	542	Hebrew Benevolent Orphan Asylum	5,000

REFORMED (DUTCH) CHURCH..$12,630.86

Reformed Dutch Church	$3,790	N. W. Protestant Reformed Dutch Church	$825
Reformed Dutch Church	6,748	True Reformed Dutch Church	123
Reformed Dutch Church	1,143		

PRESBYTERIAN...$8,363.44

Canal Presbyterian Church	$130	Harlem	$98
Church of the Covenant	652	Presbyterian Church, Houston-street	150
Mercer-street Presbyterian Church	1,280	A Presbyterian Church	150
Manhattanville Presbyterian Church	1,724	A Presbyterian Hospital	1,400
Eleventh Presbyterian Church	384	Mariners' Church	311
84th-street Presbyterian Church	540	United Presbyterian Church	292
13th-street Presbyterian Church	208	United Presbyterian Church	162
Jane-street Presbyterian Church	145	Second Reformed Presbyterian Church	140
Spring-street Presbyterian Church	414	First Reformed Presbyterian Church	191

BAPTIST..$2,760.34

Laight-street Baptist Church	$170	Berean Baptist Church	$160
Macdougal-street Baptist Church	195	Baptist Church, Madison-street	175
North Baptist Church	1,000	Olive Branch Baptist Church	100
53d-street Baptist Church	637	Harlem Second Baptist Church	209
Abyssinian Baptist Church	124		

METHODIST EPISCOPAL..$3,073.63

M. E. Church, 22d-street	$173	Greene-street M. E. Church	$315
M. E. Church	102	Jane-street M. E. Church	129
M. E. Church	421	John-street M. E. Church	255
Sullivan-street M. E. Church	208	Jane-street M. E. Church	91
Bedford-street M. E. Church	506	Sullivan-street M. E. Bethel Church	221
Forsyth-street M. E. Church	250	Second Church of Evangelical Association	300

GERMAN EVANGELICAL..$2,027.24

German and English School	$1,150	German Evangelical Church	$216
German Lutheran St. Peter's Church	470	German American School Society	131
German Lutheran Church	54		

MISCELLANEOUS..$44,065.12

N. Y. Magdalen Benevolent Society	$5,000	Mission Church, 2d-Av. 125th street	$394
Protestant Half-Orphan Asylum	3,054	Dover-street Free School	2,000
Wayside Industrial Home	3,000	Union Home and School	10,000
Turnverein School	3,800	Union Home and School	7,000
School N. Y. Juvenile Society	4,336	Lying-in Asylum, Marion-street	5,000
An Evangelical Church	300		

Grand Total...$528,742.47

schools," as the *Freeman's Journal* proposes to call them—some of them may long exist, is very possible; but the system is dead. We therefore regard all excited discussion as to the details of management of the schools as being as futile and out of date as a discussion as to the expediency of matters of township administration under the colonial government of New York. It is all very well to say we will remove the Bible from the schools; no matter how valuable the tub we throw the whale, it will not save them. The quotations our December writer gave from Catholic authorities, from the *Syllabus* down, ought to have satisfied him that "godless" schools would be no more tolerable to our Catholic rulers than schismatic ones. "If they insist," says now *The Catholic World*, "on having godless schools for their children, they can have them; we cannot hinder them." *Cannot* hinder them? But you will hinder them, if you can. Do not distrust your power. It is hard to set a limit to the ability that has already accomplished so much. For the will which is to direct it, let these recent utterances of the orthodox press, added to those quoted in the following pages, be a sufficient declaration; and let them, as they show the "conscientious conviction" of Roman Catholic minds, that any school-system not under the control of the Catholic Church is but a vestibule of Gehenna, furnish the abundant justification of Roman Catholics for refusing, whenever the question shall come to them for decision, to allow the funds of the State, even if they come from Protestant taxpayers, to be turned to such atrocious uses.

From the "New York Tablet," November 20.

The School Board of Cincinnati have voted, we see from the papers, to exclude the Bible and all religious instruction from the public schools of the city. If this has been done with a view to reconciling Catholics to the common school system, its purpose will not be realized. It does not meet, nor in any degree lessen, our objection to the public school system, and only proves the impracticability of that system in a mixed community of Catholics and Protestants.

The system of common schools, as now adopted in this country, is in the main an imitation of the system decreed by the convention which sentenced Louis XIV. to the guillotine, abolished Christianity, and declared death an eternal sleep. The object of the convention was, by a system of godless schools, to root out religion from the French mind, and to train up the French youth in absolute ignorance or unbelief in any life beyond this life, and any world that transcends the senses. If we adopt and carry out the same system, our American youth must grow up thoroughly unbelieving and godless, as the order of the Cincinnati Board of Education not directly foreshadows. Catholics will do well to be on their guard against forming alliances to help them get rid of one evil by fastening on the country another and infinitely greater evil—the very evil the forever infamous Convention sought with devilish ingenuity to fasten on France.

Exclude every sectarian exercise, and wholly secularize the schools; let them teach nothing of religion, but be confined solely to secular education; what is the result? The system is even more objectionable than before.

Let the laws permit and *encourage* the establishment of denominational schools —wherever any denomination may be sufficiently numerous to justify one—such schools to be subject, of course, to State inspection, and be required to come up to a prescribed educational standard, but to be wholly *free* in the department of religious instruction. Let such schools receive their due proportion of the public tax.

From the "Tablet," December 4.

We are not opposed to public schools supported by the State, if the State provides schools for us in which we can teach our own religion; but we are opposed to infidel, godless, or purely secular schools. So are we to infidelity, and to Protestantism, but we can only demand that, if the State chooses to tax the whole community to support common schools, it is bound to provide Catholics, and Protestants too, if they demand it, schools in which children can be educated without violation of conscience.

From the "Tablet," December 18.

So far as Catholics, acting in concert with their pastors, are concerned, there is no conspiracy in the case. We say openly, we do not believe in the system, nor in any system which does not leave us free to educate our children in our own religion; and we are strongly opposed to being taxed for the support of schools in which we cannot do it.

From the "Tablet," December 25.

We demand of the State, as our right, either such schools as our Church will accept, or exemption from the school tax. If it will support schools by a general tax, we demand that it provide or give us our portion of the public funds, and leave us to provide schools in which we can educate our children in our own religion, under the supervision of our Church.

We hold education to be a function of the Church, not of the State; and in our case we do not, and will not, accept the State as educator.

From the "Freeman's Journal," November 13.

Education is not the work of the State at all. It belongs to families, and should be left to families, and to voluntary associations. The school tax is in itself an unjust imposition.

From the "Freeman's Journal," November 20.

We tell our respected cotemporary, therefore, that if the Catholic translation of the books of Holy Writ, which is to be found in the homes of all our better-educated Catholics, were to be dissected by the ablest Catholic theologian in the land, and merely lessons to be taken from it—such as Catholic mothers read to their children; and with all the notes and comments, in the popular edition, and others added, with the highest Catholic endorsement—and if these admirable Bible lessons, and these alone, were to be ruled as to be read in all the public schools, this would not diminish, in any substantial degree, the objection we Catholics have to letting Catholic children attend the public schools.

This declaration is very sweeping, but we will prove its correctness.

First : We will not subject our Catholic children to your teacher ! You ought to know why, in a multitude of cases.

Second : *We will not expose our Catholic children to association with all the children who have a right to attend the public schools !* Do you not know why ?

There is no possible programme of common school instruction that the Catholic Church can permit her children to accept. The Catholic Church claims no power to force her instruction on the children of people not Catholic. But she resists the assumption of whomsoever to force on the little ones of the Catholic fold any system of instruction that ignores her teaching, according to which the whole of this life is to fit children, and older people, for an eternal life.

It is not we who declare so. It is the Catholic Church. In the famous " Syllabus" of modern errors condemned by the Catholic Church, and which neither bishop nor layman can dispute, without the reproach of rebellion against the Church, is the following CONDEMNED, as against faith.

" That Catholics may approve the plan for teaching youth in schools apart from the inculcation of the Catholic faith, and from the control of the Catholic faith ; while such teaching regards only, or, at least, chiefly, the mere knowledge of natural things, and the purposes of our social life here on earth."

This proposition is CONDEMNED by the Catholic Church, and *no Catholic is at liberty to hold it.* The *Express*, therefore, may understand how impossible it is for Catholics ever to come to an agreement with persons not attached to any religion, in regard to schools that *she requires to be positively, and continually, dominated by the Catholic religion.*

From the "Freeman's Journal," November 20.

The issue is not about the reading or not reading of the Bible in schools. We insist upon having this apprehended and acknowledged. Bible read, or Bible not read, in the public schools, cannot alter the objection of Catholics, obedient to their faith, against the popular method of public schools. We insist on having this recognized. It is the fact.

No Catholic, in a responsible position, will or can deny that schools, not subjected to teachers, and to a discipline under the supervision of Catholic authorities, are forbidden to Catholics for their children.

The movement to exclude the perfunctory gabbling over of some verses of the Bible at the opening of schools is not a Catholic movement. If some Catholics have engaged in it, it is as politicians, not as Catholics. They may wish to embarrass non-Catholics, and set these by the ears. In this or that town or village, if this be done, it is none of our business to interfere with it. But if it be attempted to make the whole Catholic public responsible for it, we denounce the endeavor. It is not a Catholic proceeding. For our part, we object to it, and believe it is calculated to put Catholics in a false position.

The Catholic position is so clear and simple that there is no excuse for misrepresenting it.

We do not want to force Catholic school instruction on any one.

We will not have school instruction, without the Catholic religion pervading it, forced on our children.

We do not want our neighbors to be taxed for our Catholic schools.

We Catholics do not want to be taxed for schools we do not believe in, and cannot use.

If all alike are to be taxed for the support of schools, which are not properly the business of the State, we hold that all and every portion of the taxpayers ought to have the proportion of the money so raised applied in a manner not repugnant to their convictions of what kind of schooling their children should have.

From the " Freeman's Journal," December 11.

The Catholic solution of this muddle about Bible or no Bible in schools, is— "hands off!" No State taxation or donations for any schools. You look to your children, and we will look to ours. We don't want you to be taxed for Catholic schools. We don't want you to be taxed for Protestant, or for godless schools. Let the public school system go to where it came from—the devil. We want Christian schools, and the State cannot tell us what Christianity is.

OUR ESTABLISHED CHURCH.

THIRTY years ago, a young English gentleman, whose title-page described him by the strangely composite style of "Student of Christ Church and M. P. for Newark," put forth a famous plea for the maintenance of the national Church in England and of the English Church in Ireland. The subtle dialectics, the fervid and urgent rhetoric of the work, marking "the rising hope of those stern and unbending Tories who followed, reluctantly and mutinously," the more cautious lead of Peel, maintained the loftiest views of the necessity of an ecclesiastical department in every State; and especially insisted upon the continuance of the Protestant Establishment in Ireland, when that Establishment was more odious than to-day, and to a greater proportion of the Irish people. At the moment when we write, that young scholastic-parliamentary champion of the Irish Church has become the chief of an imperial ministry, the avowed purpose of whose existence is the dis-establishment of the Irish Church. His Tory predecessor, when he carried through a measure of Parliamentary Reform so radical as almost to frighten the Manchester men, did not more squarely turn his back upon the professions, than Mr. Gladstone has upon the convictions, of a conspicuous public life; yet Mr. Gladstone's change is nothing more than the stirring of a chip in the great flood of opinion which within his time has moved in that direction over almost the whole of Christendom. These thirty years, even the last third of them, have seen some tremendous and successful blows dealt at ecclesiastical power. The advocates of a godless or at least of a churchless State have been having upon the whole quite the best of it.

See Italy, the very chief and centre of the Christian Church. When a new "liberal" constitution was devised for the Sardinian States in 1848, its first article declared "the Apostolic and Roman Catholic Religion" to be "the only religion of the State." Brave words! But they did not prevent that very State from swallowing up, within a dozen years, not merely the territories of princes who held in fee of the Holy See, but all save the barest remnant of the provinces of the See itself; as if they had not been indeed the pious gift of Constantine; as if the historic decretals were not their title-deeds. And through the whole Italian kingdom, in what plight is the holy "religion of the State" to-day? With an excommunicated king, imprisoned bishops, every rood of church property confiscated or "secularized" at a stroke, the regular clergy driven by thousands from their cloistered homes, Waldensian chapels suffered to sprout like fungi all over the peninsula, the standard of the Church upheld only by the devout but irregular men-at-arms that line the highways of the southern half of it.

Look at that Austrian Empire, which once was the "Holy Roman." Within three years the concordat with the See, sacred with more than the sanctity of a civil treaty, is abrogated; all public education wrested from the clergy, and made as secular as Cornell University; the clerical sanction no longer essential to valid marriage, nor orthodoxy to burial in consecrated ground; the Protestant Von Beust, Chancellor and almost Regent of the Empire; and every form of heresy made practically, equal before the law to the faith of the fathers and the councils.

Perhaps in skeptical France little better was to be looked for: in France, which has always had a loose way of murdering its prophets, from the time when Philip the Fair roasted the Templars; whose Church has always been less Roman than Gallican; the note of whose emblematic fowl has these many centuries roused as painful emotions in the breasts of Peter's successors as its prototype could in the saint's own bosom; which with equal hand has doled out to Catholic Church, Protestant temple and Jewish synagogue their due proportion of the public revenue, without regard to abstract religious truth. So that it can cause but a mild horror when M. Rouher exclaims, as he did but a few months ago in the Chamber of Deputies, that "the entire separation of the Church from the State is but a question of time."

Then the subjects even of "Her Most Catholic Majesty" appear to esteem that particular title as lightly as they do the private virtues that have earned for her at the hands of His Holiness the honor of the Golden Rose. What little ecclesiastical property remained from the necessities of successive Most Catholic monarchs seems sure now to be swept into the revolutionary chest; and what with Bible-importations, public prayer-meetings, and Sunday-schools, Spain seems entering upon the same career of Free Church infidelity upon which France and Italy have made such vast progress.

Add to this the late triumph in our American Spain of the same cause, represented by the half-breed republican Juarez, over the church-party of Miramon and Maximilian; to say nothing of such scattered incidents as the gradual secularizing of the State in the Swiss Cantons, and the protest against a Protestant State-Church, which was emphasized by the disruption of the Scottish Kirk, and we might fairly conclude, with the Head of the Church in his recent bull convoking the Council General of the Vatican, that the universal separation of the Church from civil government is at hand.

—"We *might* conclude." But if it were permitted to hold, with the Port-Royalists, that the Pope's infallibility does not extend to matters of fact, it would be easy to show that His Holiness has been misled by changes which for the most part are limited to the regions nearest to the Vatican. Here in this Western empire, and especially in the great commonwealth in which this Magazine is published, the old State-Church problem is receiving a new solution, under new conditions. The experiments of an irreligious State, to which there is so strong a tendency in many countries to resort, has been thoroughly tried here. It succeeded to all manner of Establishments—to a Dutch Calvinistic State in New York, to a Congregationalist State in Massachusetts and Connecticut, to an English Episcopalian State in Virginia, to a Spanish Catholic in Florida, and it has been somewhat widely regarded as a failure. In fact, many of the upholders of the old Establishments have never frankly acquiesced in their displacement. Many good reasons will be given you to-day by old citizens of Connecticut, in favor of the obsolete law by which every resident was bound to contribute to the support of the Congregational Church in his parish, *primâ facie*, and until he could show that some other body had a better right to him. And to this day public opinion in New Hampshire has not been brought to abolish that badge of ecclesiasticism in its constitution which requires the officers of the State to be "of the Protestant religion."

If, then, we were really called upon, here and to-day, to argue that the State ought to "profess religion," to maintain a Church, and to "belong" to it, we need not explore far from our front-doors to find our arguments. Certainly plenty of them can be got from good Yankees and good Protestants; and early among them we should call upon that body of single-minded clergy and laymen who met in Philadelphia lately, to heal our political disorders and establish the Deity upon a sound basis by getting a recognition of him inserted into the Federal Constitution. But whatever may be the speculative interest of this question, it is for us no longer a practical one. Circumstances, and the management of adroit churchmen and judicious statesmen have saved our excitable public the agitation of a protracted controversy upon the subject. That impartial old *croupier*, our Destiny, has ceased his droning invitation to us, " *Faites votre jeu, Messieurs.*" The wheel has turned : " *le jeu est fait;* " and almost before we guessed what was at stake, we find ready to our hand, and not yet too heavy on our neck, Our Established Church.

Recognizing, then, the just limitation of inquiry in the settlement of all questions in regard to the expediency of an Establishment ; recognizing also the probable advantages there are in accomplishing great public events in the quiet way in which this has been effected, it may be worth while to take a strictly historical and practical view of our Establishment ; what it is, and how it came.

Here, then, in this commonwealth of five million souls, the ancient Church acknowledging the jurisdiction of the Roman See, while it owns its duty of caring for the whole people, claims from one and a half to three millions within its own immediate pale. Its sacerdotal or clerical body, including under that title the fraternities and sisterhoods devoted to whatever work of charity or instruction, numbers not far from two thousand, absolved from all secular and domestic cares, consecrated to the sole service of the Church and of religion, organized in a true and stringent hierarchy which is moved like a splendid mechanism by the touch of the Primate at New York. The surface of the State is mapped out into nearly seven hundred parishes, comprised in the archdiocese of New York, and the dioceses of Brooklyn, Albany, Rochester, and Buffalo. Nor is the parochial organization of any one of these numerous divisions deemed complete until it includes, besides all needful lands, buildings, and equipments for proper religious uses, a whole educational system of free-schools for boys and girls, and select schools for such as can pay a price for a better commodity, sufficient in capacity, if not in excellence, to enable the entire Catholic population to dispense with such provision as the State may make for the instruction of youth. Into these schools are gathered, for an education

at least untainted by the reading of the Protestant Bible, not many less than a hundred thousand children. Of institutions of a higher order, whether for educational, benevolent, sanatory, or strictly religious purposes, whether called asylums, hospitals, colleges, academies, or convents, the number approaches, if it does not pass, one hundred and fifty, many of them established on a vast scale, and endowed with splendid munificence. Of the money value of this enormous landed estate, owned as it is for the most part in fee-simple by one or another of five ecclesiastics under no accountability for their ownership to any civil tribunal, no computation better than a conjecture can easily be made. The " Catholic Directory " which has furnished imperfectly the preceding data, is silent, for whatever reason, upon this point. If, however, we consider the great average size of the churches, built as they are for the finest effects of a stately ceremonial, as compared with the mere preaching-houses of the Protestant sects : the value of the well-chosen building-sites in New York and the other cities, and the immense costliness of the cathedrals and greater churches; if we add in almost every parish, the ground and buildings of the parochial and other schools ; if we roughly guess the value of the Provincial Seminary at Troy, of St. John's College at Fordham, of the Sisters' Academy at Yonkers, of St. Mary's Hospital at Rochester, of St. Patrick's Orphan Asylum on Fifth and Madison Avenues ; we may well assume that $40,000 would be a low average for churches, and $20,000 for other institutions ; and upon such a basis the aggregate worth of all this property must reach from thirty to fifty millions of dollars. Whether such an endowment, exclusive of all sources of annual revenue by public largess or otherwise, is adequate or not for the established Church of a State of five millions, is a question for the future.*

* The total " subvention," in the year 1844, to the Catholic Church in France (population, 35,000,000, almost exclusively Catholic), from the nation-

Such, then, are the numbers, the high organization, the hierarchical force of this great body; such too, and out of all proportion to the poverty of its members and the recency of its growth, its vast corporate wealth. That the Church should grow in numbers was but the plain and direct result of a series of physical causes,—the construction of our great public works, beginning with the Erie Canal, to attract the most faithful children of the Church; the Irish famine to expel them; the misgovernment of many German States, driving hither their population. That the growing Church should be provided in a reasonable degree with priests, teachers, and places for Church service, in spite of the extreme poverty of most of its members, would have followed from a less earnest zeal than they have commonly shown. But this magnificent expansion of solid wealth out of abject penury calls for some clearer illustration. Perhaps we may add our farthing-candle's ray of light.

Hardly sixty years ago the slender

al treasury, departments, and communes was $9,-000,000.

The entire endowment of the Irish Church, so soon to be disestablished, for a population of nearly 6,000,000, is valued at £17,000,000, or $85,000,-000; which includes, however, in addition to the classes of property mentioned above, the value of certain bountiful sources of revenue, capitalized upon the basis of twenty years' purchase. But the disproportionately splendid endowment of the Irish Church has been one of the chief grounds of Catholic and dissenting complaint.

The reports of various charitable institutions to the comptroller of the State, in 1868, show the following valuation of property owned by those named, over and above their indebtedness. There is no reason to believe that any of the institutions has over-estimated its own property:

Roman Catholic Orphan Asylum,
  Brooklyn...........................$161,231.43
Roman Catholic Orphan Asylum,
  New York........................ 235,000.00
St. Joseph's Asylum, New York.... 127,000.00
Society for the Protection of Roman
  Catholic Children, New York.... 205,760.09
St. Mary's Hospital, Rochester.......197,912.25

That agreeable writer, Mr. James Parton, in his sympathetic paper in the *Atlantic Monthly* for April, 1868, is of the opinion that "Our Roman Catholic Brethren" own $50,000,000 worth of lands and buildings in the diocese of New York alone. This diocese includes only the southern corner of the State, up to the 42d degree of latitude, and excludes Long Island. Mr. Parton appears to have had access to excellent sources of information.

Catholic community of the Northern States was deemed important enough to require the services of three bishops, who were thereupon established at Boston, New York, and Philadelphia. But such became, before many years, the effective operation of the physical causes just specified, that when half that time had passed, the number of adult males, of inferior intelligence, but devoted with enthusiasm to the Church, and obedient to its clergy with the docility of an ardent faith, had increased so that their influence upon public affairs, under a system which allots the same quantity of political power to the brutish man as to the enlightened, was worth considering. Nor were there wanting managers of public affairs quick to discern the uses of this instrument, if only they might get their hands upon the lever that controlled it. The way seemed short and plain. Of two great parties, one seemed made to attract, without effort and by its very nature, the suffrages of an alien class, of an abject caste, and of a Church largely held in disfavor and apprehension; for it made ostentatious and sonorous profession of its indifference to all such circumstances as qualifying the one essential fact of humanity. It was rather to the leaders of the other party, which included great numbers of those who looked askance upon alienage, lowness of degree, and Catholicity, that it seemed needful to win such votes by substantial evidences of good-will. There arose, therefore, a generous competition. What Democrats were ready to do, out of the broadness of their avowed principles, for this half-outcast body, Whig managers were eager to do by way of disclaiming the narrow prejudices confessed by thousands of their followers. If Democrats were content to acquiesce in whatever condition of affairs should be accomplished by the popular will, Whig statesmen recognized the duty of foreseeing the inevitable, and of assisting it. If all the efforts they put forth to this end, devoted and effective as they were—if the relations of subservient amity which the chief of these prescient managers had maintained for a generation, through much contumely, with that eminent prelate who governed the Church in New York—resulted in no great profit to them or their party, it may help to show that an instinctive affinity is stronger than that gratitude which is merely a sense of benefits already conferred.

Not far from the year 1847, the diligent explorer of our annual statutes will find, almost for the first time, a few donations for charitable purposes quietly stowed away in the depths of the "Act-making appropriations for the support of the government" for the current year. Here and there also begin to appear special statutes for like purposes; as for example, the Act in 1849 (chap. 279), appropriating $9,000 of money raised by general tax to the Hospital of the Sisters of Charity, in Buffalo. From this point, however, the honorable rivalry of parties was producing a like result to that which attends the not dissimilar emulation of a public auction. The bids rose one above another with a boldness which possibly was not diminished by the fact that the bidders were offering what did not belong to them. From year to year, more and larger benefactions of this class were found necessary to "the support of the government," until in 1866 they had multiplied sufficiently to be collected into a district "Charity Bill," which has been annually enacted ever since, as solicitously as if, like the English Mutiny Act, all our liberties depended upon it. At the same time, and by a movement almost precisely parallel, the yearly statute-book has been encumbered annually to a greater degree with the enactments which authorize the one for the city of New York, the other for the precisely conterminous county, the levy of such sums as the State deems adequate for municipal government, and which prescribe the general objects for which they may be expended. Exactly in like manner, there begin to be discovered in these "Tax Levy" bills, considerably less

than twenty years ago, the same germs which have fructified so bountifully in the general "Charity Bill" for the State at large. By virtue of the enactment last mentioned the State paid out during the year 1866, for benefactions under religious control, $129,025.49. Of this a Jewish society received $2,484.32 ; four organizations of the Protestant sects had $2,367.03 ; while the trifling balance of $124,174.14 went to the religious purposes of the Establishment. Looking, by way of variety, at the following year for data regarding the strictly municipal gifts for like purposes, we find from the last report of the Comptroller of the city that during 1867 there was paid to Catholic ecclesiastical institutions the sum of near $200,000, aside from what may lie hidden in a vast total of more than a million, of which the details can be found only in the report of the "Department of Public Charities and Correction." While there are other benefactions in the list, hardly any are for objects having even remotely a religious character, and not one for a sectarian object. And if the proportion thus indicated holds good in the State and civic gratuities of 1868, which exceeds, we can hardly say by how much, the princely sum of half a million,* it must be conceded that the Church is in a fair way of obtaining its own, with, perhaps, a trifle of what others might lay some claim to.

But these figures do not fully indicate the favor with which the Church has been treated by her children in official station, coöperated with as they have been by the well-disposed outside the fold.† The city of New York has certain great corporate possessions,

---

* The State Comptroller reports as paid by the State alone last year, to "Orphan Asylums, &c.," $141,328.84, and adds that this sum is exclusive of $201,000 appropriated by the "Charity Bill."

† It is in view of the constant disposition of our civil State to deal kindly and even generously by The Church that we cannot but deprecate, as needlessly irritating to non-Catholic citizens, and serving no useful purpose to the Church, such utterances as the following from the leading Church newspaper of this city. Speaking of a railroad bill lately pending before the New York Legislature, which would have necessitated the removal of St.

which, if not downright wealth to the owner under the management they have received, contain at least, like Mrs. Thrale's brewery, "the potentiality of wealth, beyond the dreams of avarice," so far as such dreams had expanded in Dr. Johnson's time. Sad stories have been hinted from time to time within these few years past, of something like scoundrelism in dealing with and get-

Peter's Church, Barclay Street, the New York *Tablet* says, in a recent number:

"We will only say that the first stone of St. Peter's Church taken down by a railroad would, in our opinion, inaugurate such riots as New York has not yet seen. This we say by way of solemn warning. Let the speculators try it, and they will find what we say is true. St. Peter's Church on Barclay Street shall not be desecrated. That time-honored fabric must stand. If the Catholics of New York cannot protect St. Peter's Church, and preserve it for coming generations of their brethren, they can do nothing. None would deplore more than we any disturbances, or tumult, in this or any other city; but we say, and say again, that an unnecessary railroad shall not run where the most dear and sacred of sanctuaries stands, while their are Catholics in New York to prevent such a desecration."

Now no one whose memory reaches back to the last year or two of the administration of our late Archbishop will have the hardihood to question the power of the ecclesiastical authorities to summon, at a single word a most ferocious mob, in front of the archiepiscopal palace. And it is not to be doubted that the silent consciousness in the minds of the public and of the authorities, that this tremendous power is held in leash every moment by our ecclesiastical rulers, does its part in securing ready acquiescence in the wishes of the Church. But we point to the unbroken record of public legislation and administration in favor of all Church interests, as an argument for adhering to peaceful processes so long as these accomplish all that every reasonable friend of our Establishment can ask. We plead with our Catholic fellow-citizen against the use of *needless* menaces that only mortify the honorable pride, and exasperate the feelings of a weaker party. Surely the events of 1863, are a sufficient warning that the sensitive feelings of our Catholic public are not to be trifled with; and those events are not so easily forgotten that the lesson of them requires to be enforced with threats. The power of the mob and the riot, has, perhaps, been providentially placed in the hands of the Church, as the natural substitute for those more spiritual weapons—the interdict and the excommunication which seem to have lost something of their ancient virtue. But this power should be held in reserve as the *ultima ratio* of the Church. There can be no good, and may be great harm, in thus drawing it unnecessarily from the armory of the Church, and brandishing it in the face of an unoffending and compliant public. The idea, in the present case, that a railroad ring, however wealthy and adroit, could stand up, in the Albany lobby, against the influence of the Established clergy, is too absurd for comment.

ting rid of these vast properties,—the ferries, docks, markets, and various blocks and tracts of land,—on the part of the New York government. It is not for us to sit in judgment upon those functionaries, nor to conjecture how much of the municipal property, so far from having stolen, they have, with the high virtue of those who let not their left hand know what their right hand doeth—who "do good by stealth, and blush to find it fame"—quietly devoted to the pious uses of the Church. But the last Comptroller's report contains, with regard to certain of the real estate which yet remains on the island of Manhattan, some interesting avowals, by which the city government is willing to let its light so shine before men that they may see its works, and glorify its father, which is—no matter where. In the schedule of city property subject to payment of ground-rent (pp. 166–169,) we find that the premises on "51st Street and Lexington Avenue" are leased to the (Catholic) Nursery and Child's Hospital; that the lease is dated April 1, 1857, is *perpetual,* and for the annual rent of One Dollar, which was three years in arrear. That the property on "81st and 82d Streets and Madison Avenue" is leased to the "Sisters of Mercy;" that the lease (the date of which is not given), is *perpetual,* and the annual rent One Dollar, which, however, had been paid until within two years of the report. That the land on "51st and 52d Streets, Fourth and Fifth Avenues," was leased April 1, 1857, to "The Roman Catholic Orphan Asylum," *perpetually,* for the annual rent of One Dollar. This sum, however, it is gratifying to observe, has been fully paid to the end of 1867.

Upon some part of this property, or upon another tract held by a like title and upon similar terms, is in course of erection the new St. Patrick's Cathedral, which is intended to be worthy of its proud rank of metropolitan church of this great commonwealth.*

* It is pleasant to find Mr. Parton, in the *Atlantic* for April, 1868, extolling the foresight of the late Archbishop Hughes in buying this tract at a

From estimates of those competent to
appraise land in New York, it appears
that these blocks alone are worth not
less than $3,000,000.* It may be con-
cluded, therefore, that the city would
get the worth of this property, if it applied every payment upon the principal,
asking nothing for interest, in about
one million years.

Thus increasingly munificent in their
provision for the maintenance of a
church-establishment have been the rulers of an American State, during a generation noted for the fiercest onslaughts,
in other lands, upon the sacred institutions of antiquity, and in which scoffers
have pretended to discover more " spiritual wickedness " than pure spirituality in the " high places " of politics.
In so extraordinary a ratio, too, has
this devout allotment of the public
revenues increased, that what in 1849
was but about $13,000 and that given
but grudgingly, is grown to not far
from $500,000, in 1868, bestowed with
the frank generosity of those who give
of others' goods. If some crabbed rustic, the slowness of whose toilsome gains
begets a narrow curiosity concerning the
manner of disposing of them, or whose
sectarian jealousy sets him against the
Church of the Commonwealth, shall
reckon that this rate of increase, far beyond the increase of the Church, will
bring the annual gift to $40,000,000 in
1918, and to $80,000,000 in 1968, we
need only smile at his hedge-philoso-
phy. It is quite enough that these
benefactions should continue upon the
scale they have now reached for a few
years longer. Every year the Church
gains upon the sects. The generation
in which we are proud to be numbered,
assumes the burden of the ages. When
our children are men and women, the
State, perhaps, will have done giving
to the Church ; perhaps it will have be-

time when other purchasers would not. But a
willingness to risk one dollar a year for a block of
lots on Fifth Avenue, any time within fifteen
years, could hardly have been deemed a wild passion for speculation.

The article referred to, and its successor in the
Atlantic for May, we may be permitted to cite *pas-
sim*, as *pièces justificatives* for this paper.

* *Probably* this is much below the present value.

gun soliciting from the Church instead.
And the wild reaction of irreligion
which seems to be sweeping on as it
has before over Christendom—the spirit
which at different times has driven
even from every Catholic country the
Society of Jesus itself—should it then
reach this favored commonwealth, will
find the Church with all its agencies,
too strongly entrenched in the benefactions of these years to be dislodged.

No State-Church, it may fairly be
said, fulfils the whole duty of its position, which fails to grasp and superin-
tend the whole system of education.
No graver charge can be brought
against the Church of Ireland or the
Church of England than that with the
enormous means at their disposal, they
have suffered such vast populations to
be born, grow old, and die, in the dead-
ly darkness of ignorance that envelops
them from the cradle to the coffin. The
Church of New York, however its enemies may malign it, will be free from
this sin. So far has it been conscious
of the duty, that it has not been content that the thing was done, unless
done by itself. The State was manag-
ing the matter in its own rude way.
Pretending, it is true, to exclude sectarian teachings, it yet required the
Bible, which, when unaccompanied by
suitable comments, is confessedly a sectarian book, to be read in its schools.
No better proof was needed that the
Church could not abdicate its duty.
Its efforts were, therefore, two-fold. It
sought to exclude sectarianism from
the public schools; it sought also to
make schools of its own which should
compete with the public ones, be maintained with the public money without
being responsible to the public, and in
time render the State schools superflu-
ous. That it does not lose sight of the
former object in the vast success of the
latter may be seen by observing the
names of candidates, at every municipal
election, for the Board of Education.
If an inborn reserve has kept back from
other positions the Celtic adherents of
the dominant faith, duty or skillful organization crowds them into these can-

didacics, if possible upon both the opposing tickets. But the grand and ultimate object of its efforts is to make schools of its own which shall crowd out by degrees the public schools, until the universality, which is the sole justification of the present scheme of public education, shall palpably appear a mere pretence of which common honesty must demand the suppression ; and in this object, dearest to the Church's heart, she has received the most efficient aid from aliens, and even from enemies. The frantic Protestantism which, when Protestants were stronger than now and Catholics fewer, screamed itself hoarse with demands that the schools should be Protestant or nothing, because Protestantism was right and "Romanism" was wrong, and because it was the duty of the majority to educate according to its convictions, has furnished all the arguments the Church can ask for, now that it is about attaining *its* majority, for demanding that the common schools shall be Catholic or nothing. And when that point is reached, if discussion shall be in order, the mouths of the ultra Protestants at least will be stopped with their own hot words. Nor did they less, when the combat was first opening, furnish the occasion for the aspiring politicians, of whom we have already spoken, to concede in the name of fairness and equity the preliminary requirements of the Catholics. That illustrious Whig who maintained *per tot discrimina* the serenity of his friendship with the Archbishop of New York, little as the Archbishop could persuade *his* friends to vote for Whig candidates, deserves the honor of having led the slow movement of events. If they have reached his early advance only after the lapse of thirty years, they have yet followed him as truly as the ultimate overthrow of the rebellion succeeded, after four years, his famous and successive predictions that it was to come "in ninety days."

In the annual Message, which ushered in the year 1839, Governor Seward is found speaking with great tenderness of our fellow-citizens of foreign birth. "We must secure to them," he says, "as largely as we ourselves enjoy, the immunities of religious worship. And we should act no less wisely for ourselves, than generously toward them, by *establishing schools in which their children shall enjoy* advantages of education equal to our own, with free toleration of *their peculiar creeds and instructions.*" If the hardness of his people's hearts in 1839 forbade their acting at once upon counsel that was too "advanced" for them, he was not dissuaded from repeating it in the Message of 1840. "The children of foreigners * * * are too often deprived of the advantages of our system of public education, in consequence of prejudices arising from difference of language or religion. * * * I do not hesitate, therefore, to recommend *the establishment of schools* in which they may be instructed by teachers speaking the same language with themselves and *professing the same faith.* * * * Occasions seldom offer for a trial of our magnanimity by committing that trust [of education] to persons differing from ourselves in language or religion."* As magnanimity is a virtue of the powerful, it may safely be said that there will be even less frequent occasion henceforth than when Mr. Seward was Governor, for its exercise by the Protestants of New York.

In 1841 and 1842, it is evident from the tones of the Messages that the public had shown itself unworthy of such a leader. The rhetorical fervor which distinguished even those early State-papers of the since renowned Premier, glows and coruscates as before from beginning to end, through facts and figures, statements of finance, canals, and commerce, the past, the present, and the future; but the easy confidence of manner is wanting in the paragraphs which relate to the establishment of Roman Catholic schools. At great length the good Governor deprecates the criticism which he has evidently incurred, and defends his innocent proposal against what seem to have been violent attacks. He had suggested nothing worse than "employing for their instruction teachers, who, from their relations toward them, might be expected to secure their confidence." For himself, he "indulged no apprehensions from the influence of any language or creed among an enlightened people." "To me (he continues), the most interesting of all our republican institutions is the Common School. I seek not to disturb, in any manner, its peaceful and assiduous exercises, and, least of all, with contentions about faith or forms."

To what degree this vehement effort of the Church, with such helpers as these to become independent of State education, has hitherto been successful, may be judged from the data already given, as well as from the stately edifices which in the parishes of every city, rival or surpass the grandeur of the State's school-houses. Nor does the Church longer stand, as once it did, in the attitude (well as the attitude becomes Christ's poor), of a mendicant at the door of the State-House, asking for gratuities toward the support of its separate schools. It has already established by action in the Supreme Court the clear legal right of its orphan asylums, numerous as they are, and liberal as they are in the degree of bereavement required for admission to their scholastic privileges, to an equal participation in all moneys raised by taxation for school purposes in the State, in proportion to their number of pupils.* It remains to be seen whether so baleful a result will ensue from this recent decision as was produced in Louisiana many years ago by a humane enactment forbidding the separation of slave children under five years of age from their parents. The number of colored orphans of less than that tender age daily advertised for sale in the New Orleans papers was such as might have appalled a humanitarian who did not know the state of the law.

Thus having begun with the demand that public schools be made rigorously secular; having then obtained that sec-

tarian schools be supported by the State, the only remaining step toward complete ecclesiasticism in education is now vehemently urged, that all secular schools shall be abolished as mere seminaries of atheism. Then, and then only, in the view of *The Catholic World*, for May, 1868, will public education be put upon its true ground ; * the ground upon which so much has been done for universal education in Italy and Spain, and from which that service has been lately dislodged with violence in Austria and France. The demand here, in short, is exactly what it is in Ireland, where, as well as here, a timid Protestant minority is trying to make what terms it can. What some one says of the attitude of the Irish Catholic bishops toward Mr. Gladstone and his ministry, might be said as correctly of the position of our New York Church. "The educational question is still plainly one of the rocks ahead, as the bishops insist on the public schools being divided amongst the different religious denominations, or, at all events, on having a certain proportion of them, or of the educational funds, handed over to the Catholic clergy ; in other words, they seek what they seek here, and would like to get everywhere, but what every government in Europe, even in Catholic countries, now denies them."

Nor is the step a long or a difficult one which separates the actual condition of affairs from the one longed for as an ultimate settlement. Even while we write, the Bill which shall do the business, having been maturely considered by the Committee of the Senate on "Charitable and Religious Societies," has been reported favorably to that body. Its first section, which contains its substance is a simple provision that "Whenever there shall be or has been established and maintained in any city of this State any free school or schools in which not less than two hundred children have been or are taught and educated gratuitously it shall be the

---

* *St. Patrick's Orphan Asylum* vs. *Board of Education, Rochester.*

* See also an article in the *American Educational Monthly*, for January, 1869, on "The Catholic View of Education in the United States."

duty of such city or of the Board of Supervisors of the county of which such city is a whole or a part, to make provision from year to year for the expenses of such school or schools."

It is not as deep as a well, nor as wide as a door; but it is enough. Only let it pass, and what the Church asks for in vain in Ireland, what it has had wrested from it in Austria and Italy, it will have once and forever in New York. Perhaps it will not pass—at this session; but the Church can bide her time. In some not distant year parties may not be so adjusted in the Legislature as now. When the day comes it may well be believed that the discrimination which provided in the last Senate that this particular committee should contain a majority of Catholics, small as was their minority in the Senate; which has provided in the present Senate that a majority should be made up of Catholics and certain allies of the Protestant name who are ready to maintain the great system of Catholic schools by public largess, on condition that their own little scheme of sectarian education may nibble at the crumbs that fall from their master's table; that such discrimination will see that the interests of religion are cared for. And whatever may be the difficulty and expense of passing the bill, it will be harder yet to repeal it.

It might, perhaps, be worth while, if any one should prefer mere superficial or external signs of supremacy, to notice a few such as may be found in the city of New York itself. Not many a State-Church in the present age imposes the test of membership as a condition to holding civil office. The Church in Austria does not; in England it has not for forty years; in France not for eighty. It does not yet in New York. How near it comes to it may be partly guessed by any one who will look over a list of New York elective officers with the discriminating sense of him who "knew the stranger was an American from his name, O'Flaherty." If the inference from nationality should be deemed illusive, because not all Irish-

men are Catholics, let it be remembered that the Catholics who are not Irish will far more than make such an error good. Such researches would show a judiciary adorned with the names of Shandley, Conolly, Hogan, and Dennis Quinn, and would lead us into very green fields of nomenclature; but some one else has prepared, from better data than mere names, the following summary of Irish office-holders as they were at the end of 1868:

Sheriff,
Register,
Comptroller,
City Chamberlain,
Corporation Counsel,
Police Commissioner,
President of the Croton Board,
Acting Mayor and President of the Board of Aldermen,
President of the Board of Councilmen,
Clerk of the Common Council,
Clerk of the Board of Councilmen,
President of the Board of Supervisors,
Five Justices of the Courts of Record,
All the Civil Justices,
All but two of the Police Justices,
All the Police Court Clerks,
Three out of four Coroners,
Two Members of Congress,
Three out of five State Senators,
Eighteen out of twenty-one Members of Assembly,
Fourteen-nineteenths of the Common Council, and
Eight-tenths of the Supervisors.

Nor would even a tabular statement of office-holders, however complete, fully illustrate the influence of Our Church upon politics, unless it could include also all those non-Catholic officers or candidates, from Justices of the Supreme Court down—or up—who find it to their interest to be liberal contributors to Catholic charities or building-funds, or promptly-paying pew-owners in one or more Catholic churches.* So far does the Church permit its favorite

* "Our Roman Catholic Brethren," who furnished Mr. Parton with his data, have slily mentioned to him this source of support. See his papers.

dogma of justification by works to extend, even to those whose words frankly deny the faith.

Nor do the officers of this great municipality, whether of the Church, or merely chosen by the Church trusting in their fidelity, fail in any way to administer its affairs entirely to the Church's satisfaction. We have seen already something of the open-handedness which has bestowed millions in value of the best lands belonging to the city in perpetuity upon the dominant Church. Not less faithfully are the minor details of civic government conducted in recognition of the broad space which separates the sects from the Establishment. The Mayor, Aldermen, and Common Council might, indeed, be grieved, should Dr. Adams of Madison Square, or Bishop Potter, or Dr. Thompson of the Tabernacle, yield to our common destiny ; but their official tears may flow only upon such an occasion as Archbishop Hughes' death ; his funeral only may be graced by the corporate presence, in countless carriages, with rich profusion of gloves and scarfs. They might well be pleased, should a new Trinity, or a new Church of the Covenant, prepare to raise its graceful outlines in grander proportions, in some new quarter ; but their ceremonial joy may only be expressed by their presence when the corner-stone of St. Patrick's Cathedral is laid upon soil which the city has granted for the purpose. As our rulers desire still to be tolerant, the sects of dissent may yet find their way to their temples, in such quiet as the streets may chance to afford them ; but to those of the Establishment alone can it be permitted to cover the pavements of a Sunday with the dense processions and the crashing brazen music of an ecclesiastical ceremony, closing the most public thoroughfares to other circulation, forbidding access to other churches that happen to be upon the route, and suspending, by their clangor and clamor, whatever services such churches may be endeavoring to conduct. It is true that by the strict letter of our hitherto unad-

justed law such proceedings are not technically permissible—as could, perhaps, be practically ascertained by stationing a brass band at the door of St. Stephen's during high mass, with instructions to play " Boyne Water " for an hour unless earlier interrupted ; but the authority which is above literal law, is evinced by the squads of uniformed police which march before the processions of the Establishment, and clear the way of mere travellers. How beautiful was that vindication of the ascendency of religion over worldly interest which was telegraphed over the country on the night of March 17 ! It had been St. Patrick's day, the patron saint of the commonwealth. A train of religious devotees, so long as to require from one to two hours to pass in unbroken column any point, commemorated the holy day by marching ; and nothing, it was announced, marred the harmony of the occasion but the crime of a carman who sought to cross the enormous line, but was terribly beaten *by the police*, so that this life was despaired of. What can have tempted the carman (who should in some way be connected with the Secular Carmen of the old Romans), to his outrage, does not appear from the report of the Associated Press. Perhaps, among the thousands whom this vast column detained from their engagement, whether to take a train or a steamer, or to take up a note at bank, or to call a physician, or to reach a death-bed, this worldly-minded man deemed his duty to his load of goods more important than the rest. But the sharp discipline that he incurred may well remind us of the scourging of the money-changers, and forbid us to despair of the republic whose defenders enforce so ethereal a spirituality even in the most tumultuous scenes of worldly traffic.*

---

* They manage these things better—or at least differently — in Catholic France. We translate Art. 45 of the *Organic Articles of the Convention* [with the Pope] *of the 26th Messidor, Year IX*. "No religious ceremony shall take place outside of the edifices consecrated to the Catholic worship, in places where there are temples consecrated to different worships."

Thus, while state-religions have been toppling, and tumbling all over Christendom; thus, in this nineteenth century of materialism and rationalism, have the people of this anciently Protestant State been settling upon eternal foundations the Holy Catholic Church. Not wilfully or consciously; "they builded better than they knew." While for the most part they were wishing, perhaps, no good to the Church of Rome, trusting, perhaps, to some intangible, "spirit of republicanism," or to some imaginary, non-existent constitutional safeguard against establishments,* they were in fact endowing it with wealth from the public treasury to an amount adequate to its new promotion, to be held and administered under circumstances of freedom and irresponsibility which might be envied in the Vatican itself. In no European country, we say it with some confidence, has the clergy of a Catholic establishment its hands more nearly closed upon the whole system of public education than here in New York. Nowhere in Europe is the hierarchy of an establishment appointed by the Papal See in such absolute independence of the civil government as here. Even in the ages called "dark," monarchs have preferred long and savage wars to submitting to the appointment of bishops in their own dominions in whose nomination they had no voice, and at this day the weakest sovereign would hardly endure it from the boldest Pope.

But if there is one thing more than another in which the Church in New York may boast itself as favored beyond its sisters in any Christian land, it is the tenure by which it holds its temporalities — those worldly possessions without which a Church might, indeed, be spiritual, but could hardly sustain its unequal conflict with carnal

powers. In this tenure of its property, more than in all else, does it find a strong grasp upon its laity, an independence of civic government which defies interference, and a perpetuity which, distinctly protected as it is by the State law and even by Federal Constitution, may laugh at threatened change. Churches before have been richer; but their wealth only tempted spoliation by governments. Before Henry VIII., the "dead hand" of ecclesiastical corporations, in spite of mortmain statutes, held half the acres in the kingdom; but it was seen that a "Reformation" would be a way of unclasping the hand, and distributing the wealth; and the "Reformation" came. The Church deemed itself rich enough in France, in 1789; in Italy, in 1849, in 1859, even so late as 1866; in Spain, in the year just passed. But in all those countries it was possible for the State, convulsed with a great idea and a great necessity, to declare these vast estates to be only entrusted to the Church for the execution of certain public duties of education or religious instruction, and by legislative act to assume at once the duties it judged to have been ill-discharged, and the funds devoted to their exercise. On the other hand, in Massachusetts, the estates which from antiquity had been dedicated to the Congregational Churches once by law established, were quietly transferred in hundreds of cases, half a century ago, to the teaching of an opposite faith, by the simple action of a numerical majority in each parish in favor of the change.

But against every one of these various forms of assault our church property here is protected by its tenure, the laws of the State, and the Constitution of the United States. There is in each parish a "Religious Society," as it is called in the statutes, with its board of trustees and everything convenient for holding property. But it holds none. It has been a convenience for the purpose of raising money; it serves still as a convenient executive organization for the performance of certain parochial

* The Federal Constitution prohibits *Congress* alone from making a "law respecting an establishment of religion." The constitution of New York contains no such prohibitions, although it seeks to secure "the free exercise and enjoyment of religious profession and worship, without discrimination or preference." Dissent is similarly protected in most European countries.

business. The owner of the church, its land, its parsonage, its school-houses, and all its multiform accessories, is the Bishop of the Diocese in which it stands. Nor must it be fancied that he owns it in an official character, such as that of the "corporations sole" of the English law; or in any legal sense as trustee, expressly or by implication. No freeholder owns his plot of ground more absolutely in his own right, without responsibility or liability to account to any man therefor, than John McCloskey owns the church-property in the Arch-diocese of New York, or S. V. Ryan that in the Diocese of Buffalo. It may well be that the long accumulating dimes of ten thousand believers have bought the ground and reared the splendid structure, while the conveyance is made to the single ecclesiastic who is overseer of a hundred flocks; but if no trust be expressed in the grant (and none ever is), none, by our law, can be implied. So far as the laws of this commonwealth affect the case, the owner of these vast estates may to-morrow sell the schools for cotton-factories, the churches for skating-rinks, and invest the proceeds in the dry-goods trade. Can a nobler tribute be paid to the fidelity of these prelates, than to cite the fact that the due administration of these many millions of property depends solely, without the protection of law, upon their personal honor, invigorated by some ecclesiastical discipline and a little private persuasion?

The simplicity of this tenure may be illustrated by an example of daily occurrence. A congregation of poor Germans in the western part of this State, having expended $50,000 in buying land and building upon it a large and beautiful church, desired to borrow the small balance necessary for its entire completion. Its priest, accordingly, makes the formal application to a Savings Bank. The abstract of this title presented for approval to the legal adviser of the Bank, shows the various parcels composing the tract centreing at last in one John Timon, who is known extrin-

sically, though nothing on the record shows it, to have been Catholic Bishop of Buffalo. Next appears the will of John Timon, devising all his property to one John Loughlin. So John Loughlin, who happens to be Bishop of Brooklyn, executes alone a mortgage upon the land and buildings to the Savings Bank; and no doubt before this has delivered to Timon's successor a quit-claim deed of all his vast estates in western New York, or else has executed a will which, like Bishop Timon's, transfers all his property at his death to some other prelate, and saves it from the doubtful orthodoxy of those who might have been his lawful heirs.

We have not spoken of the trifling part in this transaction played by the "trustees" of the corporation. Under the Act of 1863, which is one of the latest steps taken in the legalization of our State hierarchy, the function of trustees so nearly disappears, that it may safely be eliminated from the argument.

When we mention that provision of the organic law of the United States (Art. 1, Sec. 10, subd. 1,) which prohibits the interference with rights which have accrued under such arrangements as these, it becomes evident that the Church has nothing to fear either from wild spoliation as under Henry VIII., or from disestablishment on grounds of expediency as in the countries just named. Until a revolution which shall shatter the defences of the national Constitution, no earthly sovereignty has power to lay a finger upon her splendid endowments; while her security against the insidious growth of heresy within her fold, against such internal change as in Massachusetts made the ancient churches Unitarian, and in New York has made so many Congregational churches Presbyterian, is no less complete. As the parish owns nothing, the majority or the totality of the parish can be of no more avail in directing the use of church property than the fly that buzzes about the altar-candles. Outsiders, aliens to this Israel, look on with a certain interest at such an insurrection against Episcopal authority as took place the other day at Auburn. But how can the result of such conflicts, however violent or prolonged, be other than it has already been in that "Holy Family" Church—now once more a Happy Family—submission and obedience?*

Since the main question seems to be settled upon this basis, it may naturally be asked, in the language of a New York ecclesiastic to some earnest Protestant who had murmured against the actual state of things, "What do you propose to do about it?" Clearly, every citizen, whether he fancies it or not, is bound to ask himself the question, and to find an answer. We do not seek to supply the answer. We would barely suggest that many things yet remain, in our institutions, usages, and laws, that are the product of a different state of things and are incongruous with the present, and need modification and adjustment to fit the change of circumstances. Whether it might be worth while, in the absence of any existing power having the interest and the ability to counter-balance the power of the Church—one of the greatest and most useful labors of monarchs in every other Christian land—to set up some

other sovereignty than that of the impersonal "people," is a question upon which our friends of the "Imperialist" newspaper, and very likely a good many zealous Protestants, might hold the affirmative. Our own judgment would be that it is too late for any such expedient; and our only suggestions would relate to minor matters. It would no doubt be suitable, for example, if not necessary, that the supremacy of the Church should be recognized in our legal holidays. It would not be difficult to observe the 17th of March, dear as it is to the heart of New York, and cease the cold and perfunctory celebration of the 22d of February. It is already demanded that the State and National Thanksgiving shall be annually appointed for the 8th of December, which is the Feast of the "Immaculate Conception of the Blessed Virgin Mary," being "the Patronal Feast of the United States." Such things may be trifles; but difference in trifles produces discord; and discord is enmity and war. "A house divided against itself cannot stand." Even those who find it impossible to reconcile themselves to the new order of things as desirable, may yet see the necessity of deferring to it as actual and irreversible. While one large class of our citizens is rejoicing over the momentous but peaceful revolution of which we have been the dispassionate historian, can the other and dissatisfied class do better than lay to their own hearts the advice which they have lavished upon the subjugated citizens of the rebellious States, and since the change is an accomplished fact, accommodate themselves with alacrity to their new relations, and make the best of it?

---

* The inhabitants of a certain French rural commune, not many years ago, from Catholics became for the most part, by a common movement, Protestants. The church-property was at once transferred to them by the government, for Protestant service. Whatever change of opinion might occur in New York, the church might defy such an outrage against its rights of property. But if a Protestant congregation should (or a majority of it), turn Catholic, the transfer would be easy and rapid.

POSTSCRIPT.

Since this article was printed, a more diligent examination of the "Tax Levy Bills" for the city of New York, just passed by the State Legislature, discovers a provision for further aid to the Established Church of New York, which calls forth, from the friends of the Catholic religion, the most devout gratitude to the Providence that guides and overrules the movements of legislative bodies, but which has excited, among the enemies of the Church, an amount of vain rage and gnashing of teeth which it is painful to contemplate. A consciousness of the strength of their position, however, enables our State Clergy, in peaceful disregard of this foolish clamor, serenely to draw on the treasury for these truly magnificent donations, and sing the *quare fremuerunt gentes.* The provision is in the form of a clause providing for the distribution among certain private schools in this city of a portion of the general school-moneys which will amount, it is estimated, to a quarter of a million or more. It is understood that among the schools thus handsomely provided for, there is but an insignificant number that are not "sound upon" what is coming to be considered "the main question." This munificence occurred in "the tail of the session," as the most important part of the legislative term is called. There are those who, in their paltry sectarian jealousy at this noble act of religious generosity on the part of our imperial State, do not blush to say that if it had come to light earlier in the session, it would have been prevented from passing. That this danger should have been escaped, and that this important measure should, so to speak, have *dropped* into the legislature just at the only moment when it could have passed, is only one in the long chain of wonderful and mysterious providences which have attended the whole course of legislation, by which the legal establishment and public endowment of religion in our happy commonwealth has been so peacefully effected.

THE UNESTABLISHED CHURCH.

AN anonymous writer in the July number of this Magazine, in an article on "Our Established Church," which attracted no little public attention and comment, both favorable and unfavorable, was suffered to celebrate the Roman Catholic Church as substantially the Church by law established in this State of New York; to illustrate the munificence of its governmental endowments, and to glorify its quiet political supremacy. Admiring, apparently, as well the dazzling successes of that vigorous body in this commonwealth, as the shining qualities and the prudent measures which have achieved success, this presuming writer has sought to proclaim upon the house-tops what the Church would fain have continued to enjoy uncriticised in cloistered seclusion. So averse is the apostolic spirit, from Peter, the first Pope, down through Gregory VII. and Innocent III. and Leo X., and all the gentle category, to a bald ostentation where the welfare of the Church is not to be advanced by it, that we might well have guessed that so zealous an advocate was but a volunteer whose client would soon step forward into the forum, disclaim his authority, and decline to be concluded by his facts or arguments.

Precisely this is what has occurred. The Church of which this contributor assumed to write has other ways of expressing itself than through anonymous writers in journals not avowedly Catholic; and it has promptly and efficiently spoken to disavow the pretensions which he has put forth for it, and to denounce him with some portion of the severity which he seems to have deserved. We herein undertake to show, from the highest Catholic authority, how great were the errors of the article entitled "Our Established Church," published in this Magazine last July. We may premise, too, that out of much concurrent and competing testimony, we select our refutation mainly from two sources: (1). The letter which the Bishop of Rochester (we are almost compelled to add *in partibus infidelium*, from his statement of the position the Church occupies), addressed to a local newspaper, and through it—*urbi et orbi* —to that city and the world; and (2.) *The Catholic World* for August, in its leading article, entitled, like the paper to which it was a reply, but apparently, unlike that, in an ironical spirit, "Our Established Church." The authority of a great ecclesiastical dignitary, like that of the chief magistrate of a State, is too high to need certification from any body; above all men, a Bishop speaks *ex cathedrâ*, even when he sends his pastorals to a printing-office. Nor can the oracular character of *The Catholic World* any more be brought in question, bearing as it does upon its very cover the *imprimatur* of the Archbishop and Primate of New York, of the Cardinal Prefect of the Propaganda, and of His Holiness Pope Pius IX. himself. We shall venture, therefore, after presenting from these authorities the confutation of the article referred to, to proceed to exhibit from the same unquestionable sources the actual position of the Church of Rome in this country in relation to the sects which surround it and the State in which it exists.

The more painful part of the duty which we have undertaken—the contradiction of actual misstatements of fact- is in a measure relieved by the discovery that, as the result of the very sharp criticism which has been applied to the article in question by so many unfriendly eyes, they are discovered to be no more than two, or possibly three, in number, and of no darker enormity than these :

1. The site of the new Cathedral was included, by an error of topography, in

the magnificent grants of adjoining property from the city to the Church.

2. By a like blunder the non-Catholic "Nursery and Child's Hospital" was confounded with the Catholic Orphan Asylum hard by.

We decline to admit the plea, which might be made in behalf of these misstatements, that the block next north of the Cathedral was the gratuitous gift of the Common Council; that it is but a step along Fifty-first-street from one to the other of the children's asylums thus referred to; and that the Catholic one is, in fact, a beneficiary in the manner thus charged. Nor shall we admit as extenuation any such straggling paragraphs as this, produced from a late newspaper—

" The sum of $8,928.84, due for assessment, has been donated by the New York Common Council to St. Patrick's Cathedral."

—for what the city does toward building the church does not go to show that it gave the land for it. But with some misgivings lest the case may only be injured by such persistence, we venture to repeat this story about the details of the Orphan Asylum business, to which an air of authenticity is given by the references to the public records.

It seems, then, according to this story, that in Book "A" of Deeds in the Comptroller's Office, at p. 271, is recorded a deed, with a "covenant for quiet enjoyment," from "The Mayor, Aldermen, and Commonalty of New York" to "The Roman Catholic Orphan Asylum Society" (John Hughes, President), in that city. The consideration expressed is One Dollar; the premises are described as bounded north and south by Fifty-second and Fifty-first streets, west by Fifth Avenue (200 feet), and extending easterly from Fifth Avenue four hundred and fifty feet; being a tract of between two and three acres, and containing thirty-six city lots. Inasmuch, however, as the writer now put to the question had never alleged a deed conveying full title to corporation property, but only leases upon rents reserved, we peremptorily object to the

statement of this instrument as being the introduction of new and irrelevant matter.

In the same office, however, in the "Book of Special Leases," at p. 134, is recorded a lease of the same date with the deed just mentioned, by which the grantors in that instrument lease to the same Society the premises bounded by Fifty-first and Fifty-second streets, east by Fourth Avenue, and west by the tract just described, "during the pleasure of the party of the first part and their successors," for the yearly rent of One Dollar. This property is 200 feet by 375, or thirty city lots, and is very cheap at a dollar a-year, but for the precarious tenure at the pleasure of the Corporation. This defect, however, which at the worst it was hypercritical to object to, was soon corrected. By resolution of the Common Council, October 21, 1857, the Comptroller was directed to lease the plot to the Society "so long as it shall be occupied for the use of the Asylum," at the same rent of One Dollar a-year. The lease executed in pursuance of this resolution bears date December 31, 1857, and has been on file in the Comptroller's office since May 11, in the year memorable for Orphan Asylums, 1863.

This particularity, regarding only one, it is true, of the statements in controversy, certainly appears plausible. But as we read in *The Catholic World* (p. 583) that "only one such lease, that for the House of Industry for the Sisters of Charity, has been made in this city since 1847," we are forced to conclude that the records are mistaken, thanking that magazine at the same time for the mention of the lease for the "House of Industry," which the article in PUTNAM had somehow omitted to notice. How many and how serious are the similar omissions, we very likely shall never know; for the ways in which these things are done are various and inscrutable; and many things which an outsider may search for in vain, the authorities of the Church can publish or keep silent, as they choose.

3. The third and only remaining

error found in the paper in question, aside from the fundamental and pervading error of declaring the Church lawfully established and adequately endowed, consists in the statement that the landed estate of the Church, valued at fifty millions or more, is owned in great part " by one or another of five ecclesiastics." The Bishop of Rochester avows himself to be "one of the five . . holding property," and proceeds to add that he holds no property, but that a good deal in his diocese is held instead by another of the five, the Bishop of Brooklyn. We fail to grasp the special importance of this correction; it is enough that Bishop McQuaid has made it. The additional statement, that the four owners of church property are engaged in transferring it, more or less at their leisure, to the religious societies organized under the Act of 1863, deserves, however, even to our minds, fuller explanation; and the same explanation will serve to show why it was that the successors of the Apostles have been obliged hitherto, like the Apostles themselves, to add to "the care of all the churches" the charge of their temporalities.

Before 1863, the law of religious societies in this State was a general one, making no distinction between Catholic, Methodist, or Hicksite Quaker congregations. In all such organizations alike, the parishioners who attended the worship, who paid for the land, the buildings, and the service, were intrusted with the control of what they paid for. With this arrangement the sectaries, of whatever schism, are still forced to content themselves; but it hardly needs a bishop to explain that it is incompatible with the spirit of the Catholic Church. In 1863, therefore, a year propitious for such enterprises, as this city attested at midsummer, the existing Act was passed (Laws of 1863, chap. 45), applying, by its express terms, only to Roman Catholic congregations. It provides that in every parish which chooses to organize under it, the corporate body shall consist of five trustees. These are the Bishop or Archbishop of the diocese, the Vicar-General of the diocese, the Pastor of the church, all "for the time being," and "by virtue of their offices;" and two laymen, members of the church, appointed by the other three, and holding their places for one year. The Vicar-General and Pastor may be removed and replaced by others, at the will of the Bishop, without a moment's notice; the two laymen are removable every year, at the option of the other three, or a majority of them. A better arrangement to prevent the evils of divided councils it is difficult to conceive of; nor is it greatly to be wondered at that Bishop McQuaid should be willing, as he says, to put the title to the lots on which he is "building the Bishop's house" "in the name of St. Patrick's Church Society,"—of whom, he might add in the sententious manner of Artemas Ward, "I am which." The magnificent structure of hammered stone, in size and splendor, if not in name, a palace, which is fast rising upon those lots, will no doubt be managed quite to the satisfaction of its occupant; and as the Bishop, we understand, notwithstanding what a stranger would infer from the extent of his new mansion, is not a man of family, he cannot but be content with the absolute control for life of all his estate, and its undisturbed transfer at his death (may it be distant!) to his successor.

When it is observed, moreover, that the entire process for incorporating any Roman Catholic congregation *now or hereafter* existing, is, that the three clergymen named select their two laymen, that the five sign, acknowledge, and file a certificate showing the name of the proposed body corporate, and that "*thereupon*" such church or congregation" becomes "a body corporate," no other member of the congregation than those two needing to know one word about it until it is done, it becomes easier to understand why bishops, as well as Catholic journals, prefer their existing conveniences to any "established" arrangements that have yet been contrived.

Having thus clearly exhibited the errors into which this writer has fallen, it remains only, before setting forth to our readers such positive results as may be collected from the authorities quoted, to complete our demonstration of the main sin of inference and conclusion of which he has been guilty. The Church of Rome, then, is NOT by law " established " in this State, and the writer might have known it without waiting for the sharp admonition of *The Catholic World*, or the Rochester rappings his knuckles have incurred from Episcopal visitation. Not that the fact, upon which that journal insists so strenuously, that the Catholics are only a minor part of the population, has really any thing to do with the question. A church-establishment is only the more oppressive where its adherents are but a minority. The Established Church in England is the Church of less than half the people, and is bad enough, God knows; but the same establishment in Ireland was the Church of but a petty fraction, and does not appear to have been the less an establishment for that. The Established Church is vastly in the minority in Wales; and from the Scotch Establishment more than half the people are Dissenters. But though the thing may be possible enough, we need at present only confess that it is not actual. A simple reference to the Constitution and the General Statutes of this State would have shown this writer that the word " Established," or " Establishment," in connection with the Catholic Church, or the phrases " State Church," or " Religion of the State," are nowhere to be found. With such assurances, then, from such authorities, capped with this final argument, we leave this " sensational writer," whom " even the anti-Catholic *Nation* has rebuked for his levity," to such comfort as his schismatic conscience may allow him, for the imposture he has practised upon this Magazine, the Church, and the *World*.

Deducing now, from the lectures the Bishop and *The Catholic World* have read us, such substantial lessons as they seem to teach, we find following closely in logical order upon the primary fact that the Church of Rome is not established here, some measure for determining how much that Church lacks of being even fairly tolerated. So far from having been the object of special favors or lavish benefactions from the governing bodies in the State, its special distinction is found in the oppressive discrimination with which hitherto Legislatures and Common Councils have withheld from it all but the barest fraction of what equity and equality entitle it to. In establishing a proposition so conflicting with the pretensions put forth in the July number, it is not insisted that any part of its statistics of public largess to the Church is incorrect. Exception is taken, indeed, in the following form, to the estimate mentioned below :

" The *Magazine* [PUTNAM'S] asserts ' the State paid out, in 1866, for benefactions under religious control, $129,025.49, . . . of which the trifling sum of $124,174.14 went to the religious purposes of the Catholic Church. We have not been able to find a particle of proof of this, and the mode of reckoning adopted by PUTNAM is so false, and its general inaccuracy is so great, that in the absence of specific proof we must presume it to be untrue, and made only for a sensational effect."

Now we concede the propriety of discrediting a specific statement by alleging that the author is obviously in the habit of saying the thing that is not, and then using the statement thus discredited to impugn his general veracity. But since the statement, as we have already said, is not distinctly denied, and as it really will not affect the general argument, it may do no harm to mention, as the July writer's voucher for his assertion, the Annual Report of the Comptroller of the State for the year 1866, at pp. 71 to 75. And to show that the writer did not, as *The Catholic World* intimates, mistake such names as " The Five Points Gospel Union Mission," or " The Young Men's Christian Association " as belonging to " Catholic Institutions," we subjoin the official list of their names and the amounts of their subventions, so that,

the Protestant and Jewish being noted
by *italics*, it may be judged in how
many instances he has erred in his classification.*

But it is not necessary, it seems, to
dispute a single item of the contributor's avowedly fragmentary list of public benefactions to the Catholic Church,
in order to show with what impious
cruelty politicians have combined to
persecute that Church, to trample it
under foot, to deprive it of its just
rights. Concede that every one of the
legislative and municipal grants alleged
by the "sensational writer" has really
been made; so far from proving favoritism to the Church, they fall immeasurably short of what that Church is entitled to, and what *The Catholic World*
now squarely demands. The whole
estimate of the writer in PUTNAM is

based upon a radical misconception
of the relation of the Catholic Church
to all other religious bodies, and of the
comparative relations of that Church
and each of such bodies to the State;
a misconception, however, largely prevalent without the pale. "In this matter," it seems, "the Protestant mind
proceeds upon a sad fallacy. . . While
they call all grants and donations to
Catholic institutions sectarian, they call
none sectarian of all that [are] made
to Protestant institutions which are
not under the control and management of some particular denomination
of Protestants; . . but this is a grave
error, and cannot fail to mislead the
public. *All grants and donations made
to institutions,* charitable or educational,
*not under the control and management of
Catholics, are made to non-Catholics;*

* §

9 03	*Evangelical Lutheran, St. John's Orphan Home, Buffalo.*
346 04	Free School of the Academy of the Sacred Heart, Manhattanville.
24 62	Le Couteulx, St. Mary's Deaf and Dumb Asylum, Buffalo.
500 00	Do., Special Appropriation.
777 59	*Orphan's Home and Asylum of the Protestant Episcopal Church, New York.*
1,304 87	*Protestant Half Orphan Asylum, New York.*
2,189 21	Roman Catholic Orphan Asylum, Brooklyn, 1864.
2,576 74	Roman Catholic Orphan Asylum, Brooklyn, 1865.
4,340 63	Roman Catholic Orphan Asylum, New York.
2,505 71	Society for the Protection of Destitute Roman Catholic Children, New York.
310 52	St. John's Catholic Orphan Asylum, Utica.
1,007 43	St. Joseph's Orphan Asylum, New York.
313 90	St. Joseph's Male Orphan Asylum, Buffalo.
9 25	St. Joseph's German Roman Catholic Orphan Asylum, Rochester.
26 21	St. Mary's Orphan Asylum, Canandaigua.
89 40	St. Mary's Boys' Orphan Asylum, Rochester.
423 04	St. Mary's Orphan Asylum, Dunkirk.
238 75	St. Patrick's Female Orphan Asylum, Rochester.
180 07	St. Vincent's Female Orphan Asylum, Troy.
766 63	St. Vincent's Orphan Asylum, Albany.
267 62	St. Vincent's Female Orphan Asylum, Buffalo.
104 11	St. Vincent's Infant Asylum, Buffalo.
213 90	St. Vincent's Male Orphan Asylum, Utica.
345 51	St. Vincent de Paul Orphan Asylum, Syracuse.
118 42	*The Church Charity Foundation, Brooklyn,* 1864.
156 22	*The Church Charity Foundation, Brooklyn,* 1865.
448 72	Troy Catholic Male Orphan Asylum.
500 00	St. Mary's Orphan Asylum, Clifton. (Special Appropriation.)
1,000 00	St. Joseph's Male Orphan Asylum, Buffalo. (Special Appropriation.)
1,000 00	St. Vincent's Male Orphan Asylum, Utica. (Special Appropriation.)
8,949 84	Buffalo Hospital, Sisters of Charity.
1,646 10	Buffalo St. Mary's Lying-in Hospital.
2,484 32	*Jews' Hospital, and Hebrew Benevolent Society, New York.*
8,845 14	Rochester St. Mary's Hospital.
2,000 00	Rochester St. Mary's Hospital. (Additional Special Appropriation.)
500 00	Providence (R. C.) Lunatic Asylum, Buffalo.
1,000 00	Buffalo St. Mary's Lying-in Hospital. (Additional Special Appropriation.)
1,000 00	Church of the Immaculate Conception, New York.
2,000 00	St. Mary's Church and School, New York.
1,000 00	St. Bridget's Church School, New York.
78,500 00	The Society for the protection of Destitute Roman Catholic Orphan Children (Special Donation, Chap. 647, Laws of 1866.)

$130,025 49

and, with the exception of those made to the Hebrews, to Protestant institutions. There are but two religions to be counted, Catholic and Protestant.* The true rule is to count on one side whatever is given to institutions under Catholic control and arrangement, and on the other side all that is given for similar purposes to ALL the institutions, whether *public or private, not* under Catholic control and management ; " it being of no consequence, let it be observed, whether there is *any* religious control whatever, whether simple atheism or blank indifferentism governs them, or whether they are the ordinary non-religious institutions of the State itself. In all these cases alike they must be treated as Protestant concerns, and the payments to them countervailed by corresponding subsidies to the Catholics. Inquiring upon this solid and comprehensible basis, the *World* finds " that the total of grants made by the State to charitable and other institutions,—including the New York Institution [for] the Deaf and Dumb, the New York Institution for the Blind, the Society for the Reformation of Juvenile Delinquents of New York, *State* Agricultural College, *State* Normal School,

* We trust we shall be pardoned for intruding into the province of a theological rather than a literary Magazine, by expressing our misgivings lest the use of this argument should prove to be a polemic mistake on the part of Our Roman Catholic Brethren. It may be very true—we are inclined to think that it is—that there is a substantial religious unity in Protestantism, and that its divisions are really analogous to the divisions among Roman Catholics, representing diversity in unity. But then the contrary argument has often been found extremely convenient and effective by Catholic disputants—that Catholicism is one, and Protestantism a mere jangle of diversities. We have our fears lest the position here taken, that Protestantism is not many religions, but one, and Catholicism another, may involve the loss of a more important position in another part of the defences. It may seem absurd in us to teach any thing of the arts of controversy to such notable experts. It is like the rhetorician who lectured Hannibal on the art of war ; or like the youth who attempted to enlighten an aged relative on the method of getting at the contents of an egg through a very slight perforation of the shell. We presume that some way will be suggested of getting over the difficulty and holding both the opposite positions at once. But suspecting that possibly the difficulty might have been overlooked, we thought no harm in suggesting it.

the [*State*] Western House of Refuge for Juvenile Delinquents, *State* Lunatic Asylum, the [*State*] Asylum for Idiots, the Willard [*State*] Asylum for the Insane, academies, orphan asylums, &c., hospitals, &c., colleges, universities, &c.. and *miscellaneous*, have amounted, for twenty-one years, ending with 1867, to $6,920,881.91. Of this large amount, Catholics should have received for their institutions certainly not less than one million. Yet all that *we have been able to find* that they have received out of this large sum is a little less than $276,-000 ; that is, not over one fourth of *what they were entitled to ;* yet PUTNAM'S MAGAZINE has the effrontery to pretend that our Church is favored at the expense of Protestantism." No wonder then that Catholics, in the language of the *World*, denying that they have " received any thing like their proportion," now " *demand* for their institutions their proportion of the subsidies granted," upon the grand and simple basis of computation already laid down. Nor is this demand, founded as it is in equity, and backed by all the moral and material influences which that great body knows so well how to wield at proper moments, one which parties or people can afford to slight. The day of reckoning appears to be come ; the bill is presented for payment ; and the State will have cause for self-gratulation if the tremendous footing runs no further back than the twenty-three years which show so grievous a debit side of the account.

But this, unfortunately for the State, is very far from showing what Signor Mantilini describes as " the demnition total." And it evinces a mature confidence on the part of the Catholic Church in its secure (though unestablished) position ; that its avowed and most accredited mouth-piece should be willing to arouse the most sensitive prejudices of all non-Catholic citizens by bringing in already its little bill for the injuries it has suffered from that form of oppression, most dear to the average American, known as the Common-School System. Hereupon, we have two lessons to learn from *The Catholic World:* First, the measure of compensation necessary to make good the pecuniary damage to the Church from the inequality of our administration hitherto; Second, the form of rearrangement which the Church now demands, insists upon, and without which it refuses to be at peace with the State.

After the impressive tabulation we have just repeated, the *World* goes on:

"But we have not yet stated the whole case. We do not know how many millions are appropriated annually for the support of public schools throughout the State; but in this city the tax-levy, this year, for the public schools, is, we are told, $3,000,000, or over. Catholics pay their proportion of this amount, and they are a third of the population of the city. . . . *The public schools* are anti-Catholic in their tendency, and *none the less sectarian because established and managed by the public authority of the State.* . . We count in the grants and donations to Protestant institutions, *the whole amount raised by public tax,* together with that appropriated from *the School Fund* of the State for the support of the public schools. Thus we claim that Catholic charities and schools do not receive, in grants and donations, *a tithe* of what is honestly or justly their share, whether estimated according to their numbers, or according to the amount of public taxes for sectarian, charitable, and educational purposes levied upon them by the State and its municipalities." *

---

* The wrong done by the July contributor was in estimating the various appropriations and grants to the Catholic Church as mere gifts, rather than as "payments on account" of a just and righteous debt, the overwhelming total of which is hardly diminished, in a perceptible degree, even by these magnificent contributions. Taking the estimate of *The Catholic World,* we present its careful and unprejudiced views of the financial relations of the State to the (unestablished) Church for a single year, in a form which will be clear to business men, and which will show that under the show of liberality we have really been treating her with the most shameful injustice.

THE STATE OF NEW YORK, TO THE HOLY ROMAN AND APOSTOLIC CHURCH, DR.

To a due proportion of grants and donations to Charities and Schools, 1866, being ten times the sum actually paid.	$1,251,741.40

CR.

By cash, being less than "a tithe of what is honestly and justly their share,"	125,174.14
Balance still due for 1856. .	1,126,567.26

In view of this lucid statement of the rights of the Catholic Church, language fails us fitly to characterize the passion or folly of those who would represent, as did the writer of "Our Established Church," that the subsidies heretofore bestowed upon that body indicate that it "is in a fair way of obtaining its own." When we consider how vast are the sums consecrated (we use the word in its French sense) during the past thirty years to the American scheme of public education, and remember that every dollar was spent in downright hostility to the Roman Church, and as truly for sectarian purposes as if it had gone to pay the salaries of Methodist ministers, we may well conclude that all the benefactions brought together by the offending writer are less than "a tithe" of the just claims of the Church, or of what it now demands. Is there a politician in the State who will oppose the liquidation of so just a debt?

But even more valuable than the mere financial computation is the information the *World* gives us as to the terms upon which the vexed question of common schools may be permanently adjusted. It is a mistake, in the first place, to suppose that Catholics have any objection to the system "for non-Catholics. If they wish the system for themselves, we offer them no opposition. . . . We oppose it not when intended for them, but only when intended

---

We will not undertake to compute the interest to date. These revelations (for we confess they are such to us) of the way in which the State of New York has been running behind, year after year, in its "honest and just" debts, are simply appalling. Damaging as this statement may be to the market value of State securities, we thank *The Catholic World* for bringing it to the notice of our public financiers. *Pay as you go* is a good motto for States, as well as individuals, in dealing with any creditor. But there are three sorts of creditors in whose case it is specially appropriate— the Water company, which, in default of payment, stops your water supply; the Gas company, which turns off your light at the street main; and the Church, which cuts off your sacramental grace. When complete religious liberty is established, at last, and the Church is in a position to enforce her "honest and just" claims against the State, these monstrous arrearages of more than a million a-year will put the latter at a terrible disadvantage.

for us, and we are taxed to support it." The ground of objection is, that there can be no proper education which is not religious, and that education belongs therefore not to the State, but to the Church. This opinion amounts, with Catholics, to a "conscientious conviction." "Whether we are right or wrong, is no question for the State or civil authority to settle. The State has no competency in the matter. It is bound to respect and protect every citizen in the free and full enjoyment of the freedom of his conscience. We stand before the State on a footing of perfect equality with non-Catholics, and have the same right to have our Catholic conscience respected and protected, that they have to have their non-Catholic and secularized conscience respected and protected. We do not ask the State to impose our conscience on them, or to compel them to adopt and follow our views of education; but *we deny its right* to impose theirs on us, or *even to carry out their views of education in any degree at our expense. The Catholic conscience binds the State itself* so far, but only so far, as Catholics are concerned. . . *Its only just and honest course* is to abandon the policy of trying to bring both together in a system of common schools. . . . As both are equal before the State, it can compel neither to give way to the other. This may or may not be a disadvantage; but it is *a fact*, and *must* by all parties *be accepted* as such." If the State "will, as it is bound to do, respect and protect the rights of conscience, or real religious liberty, the only solid basis of civil liberty, it must do as the continental governments of Europe do, and divide the public schools into two classes; the one for Catholics, and the other for non-Catholics. . . . Let the State appropriate to Catholics, for the support of schools approved by their Church, their proportion of the School Fund, and of the money raised *by public tax* for the support of public schools. . . . This, if the State, for public reasons, *insists* on universal education, is the best way of solving the difficulty. . . Another way

would be, to exempt Catholics from the tax levied for the support of the public schools, and give to the schools they maintain their proportion of the School Fund held in trust by the State, and leave Catholics to establish and manage schools for their own children in their own way, under the supervision and control of the Church. Either way of solving the difficulty would answer our purpose, and we venture to say that *one or the other method* of dealing with the public school question will ere long *have to be* adopted, *whatever the opposition excited.*"

Let it be assumed now that all the proposed statistics of the contributor in regard to public largesses are not only correct, but are far below the actual facts; they would yet be vastly inferior to this authentic announcement of the demands and determined purposes of the Catholic Church, in significance to the people of this and of all these United States. Right or wrong, the system of free, public, universal education, which has been developed from the Puritan germs planted in New England into the various forms, of identical essence, in which it exists to-day in every Northern State, is immeasurably precious to the American heart. Growing up as it did in the midst of sects warring certainly not less bitterly than now, controlled, no doubt, in its infancy in some Eastern States by the religious bodies which until lately were "established" there, it has yet been fortunate enough to endure to a lusty and symmetrical maturity, which has enforced respect and immunity from contending factions. Nor is there wanting to non-Catholic citizens, of whatever creed, an enthusiasm of devotion to their school-system, an unquestioning faith that it is a principal cause of our material prosperity, and moral as well as mental eminence, and that without it our retrogression must be certain and swift, which amounts, quite as strongly as the Catholic view now presented, to a "conscientious conviction." It may be that before the controversy is adjusted upon either basis which our Roman Catholic brethren lay down as the only alternatives for "solving the difficulty" raised by themselves, a Protestant conscience may assert its "rights" and demand their enforcement by the State. There is a non-Catholic conscience, we have been told, which holds as fervidly to the duty of the State to educate all its youth, as the Catholic conscience to the duty of the Church to prevent the State from doing it. Right or wrong, perverted or corrupted as a Protestant conscience may be, we have heard it said, by those to whom modern history seemed familiar, that it has often been firm, resolute, enduring to the loss of all that made life dear and of life itself, under the sharpest tests the Catholic Church has found occasion to subject it to. This Magazine is not an organ of non-Catholics; it does not undertake to assert, except as on the authority of *The Catholic World*, what "must" be done, or "*will have to be*" adopted by the State. But it is no arrogation of authority to say, what every breeze bears upon its wings, that a successful blow at the American system of common schools would thrill millions of non-Catholic souls like a sacrilege. Still less do we pretend to say that the zeal of Protestants would be more effectual to-day in protecting their school-houses, than it has been many a time before in saving their meeting-houses. We shall hardly look for greater earnestness or devotion than such as proved a poor defence to the followers of Huss and Ziska, of Coligny and Zwingli. But futile as "the opposition excited" may be, futile as *The Catholic World* assures us it will be, we look for no noiseless contact when "the Catholic conscience" which must "bind the State" comes in collision, as it moves to the overthrow of common schools, with the Protestant conscience which is bound to maintain them.

Possibly some one, Catholic or not, as unauthorized as the late writer in Putnam, may dispute our authority for saying that the Catholic system demands the overthrow of the school-system, and may endeavor to accommodate the alternatives of the *World*—the support of Church-schools by public taxation, or the exoneration from school-taxes of all who under that inducement choose to call themselves Catholics—to the continued existence of common schools. It is true that the *World* appears to contemplate the continued existence of "secular schools" under State control,—continued, when the State has cut itself off from revenues for their support, or is engaged in subsidizing private schools up to a destructive rivalry. *How long* the *World* considers that the State would act as the agent of religious sects to collect money and distribute it among them; or on the other hand would attempt to carry on the partial task of educating, not all children, but Protestant children, or finally the children only of such parents as should ultimately neglect to exempt themselves from taxation by setting up conscientious scruples, that able journal does not take occasion to remark. We respect its acuteness quite enough to presume that it believes, as we do, that it would not be long.

But the *World* refrains from saying, what we feel bound to add, that no Catholic can look with tolerance upon the continuance even of a mutilated and crippled common-school system. Relieved though he may be as a Churchman from its atheism, as a tax-payer from its cost, he continues responsible as a citizen and voter for its existence. How can the Assemblyman from St. Peter's in Barclay-street vote for the bill by which even Protestants are taxed to sustain a system of which Archbishop McCloskey says that its workings, "as far as Catholic children are concerned, have proved, and do prove, highly detrimental to their faith and morals;" and the Bishop of Newark that "it is the greatest enemy of the Catholic religion and of all dogmatic truth?" Will he not, must not every legislator, so much being granted, accept the principles laid down by the *Tablet:* "Education itself is the business of the spiritual society alone, and not of secular society. The instruction of children and youth is included in the Sacrament of Orders, and the State *usurps* the functions of the spiritual society when it turns educator. . . The organization of the schools, their entire internal arrangement and management, the choice and regulation of studies, and the selection, appointment, and dismissal of teachers, belong *exclusively* to the spiritual authority." If he turns to the *Catholic Telegraph* of Cincinnati, the honest legislator will find his last doubt resolved, for he will find, by the authority of Archbishop Purcell, that the education of common schools is "elementary instruction in atheism and immorality." "Halls of learning that are irreligious, because no particular religion is taught, must become the prolific sources of national iniquity. The secular school-system is a social cancer, presaging the death of national morality, devouring the little sense of religion that Protestantism instils into its believers. *The sooner it is destroyed the better.*" "It will be a glorious day for Catholics in this country when, under the blows of justice and morality, *our school-system will be shivered to pieces.* Until then, modern Paganism will triumph."

But we need not call in the inferior evidence of newspapers and archbishops, when the solemn declarations of the Holy See itself are so clear and conclusive upon this very point: "*Melius est petere fontes quam sectari rivulos.*"

Until the American Church ceases to be a dependency of the Roman Church, it cannot discard or evade the infallible authority of the Roman Bishop. If any American Catholic should seek to reconcile himself with American principles of education, let him hear how those principles, as expressed below, are denounced by the present Pope. The quotation is from the famous "Syllabus," or catalogue of "The Principal Errors of our Time," appended to the Encyclical of December 8, 1864:

"45. That the entire direction of public schools in which the youth of Christian States are educated, save an exception in the case of Episcopal seminaries, may and must appertain to the civil power, and belong to it so far that no other authority shall be recognized as having any right to interfere in the discipline of the schools, the arrangement of studies, the taking of degrees, or the choice and approval of teachers.

"47. That the most advantageous conditions of civil society require that popular schools open without distinction to all children of the people, and public establishments destined to teach young people letters and good discipline, and to impart to them education, should be freed from all ecclesiastical authority and interference, and should be fully subjected to the civil and political power for the teaching of matters and opinions common to the times.

"48. That this manner of instructing youth, which consists in separating it from the Catholic faith and from the power of the Church, and in teaching it above all a knowledge of natural things and the objects of social life, may be perfectly approved by Catholics."

But, however it may have been in 1864, the American Catholics of 1869 are reasonably free from all these errors.

In this same Cincinnati, which includes—we can hardly say contains—the *Telegraph*, progress is reported. The newspapers have been busy with the details of recent negotiations between the Board of Education and "the authorities of the Catholic schools," which have reached a certain result. The result is not much; mainly that "no religious teaching," or the use "of any religious books, papers, or documents [notably the Bible] shall be permitted in" the public school-houses. Naturally, this contents neither the *Telegraph* nor the *Freeman's Journal* of this city, both of which denounce the capitulation as a Catholic surrender. But their inflammation is surely unreasonable, and might be injurious if a heated journal were as dangerous to a great cause as to a railroad-train. It is much that the Church is treated with, at last, as coördinate with the State, as having belligerent rights, and as being capable of concluding compacts. From this to final success, the way is short and smooth. "*Chateau qui parle, femme qui écoute, va se rendre.*" Common Schools, good-bye!

We proceed now to a more pleasing part of the task which the temerity of this contributor has forced upon us. We rescue from the comparative obscurity to which the necessarily restricted circulation of *The Catholic World* might have condemned it, the definition which the highest literary authority, backed by the highest hierarchical authority, in the American Church, puts upon the great watchword, Religious Liberty. Here, where the Church, though not "Established," feels called upon to disavow its desire to be, because it can do better; where its public subventions, although they amount thus far to less than the tenth of its just demands, have reached an annual sum which strikes tax-payers with dismay; where its foot is upon the neck of legislatures, its grasp upon the throttle of all public education, it becomes a question of more than speculative curiosity, when the Church is heard to speak respectfully of "religious liberty," what it means by the phrase. When the Church "shall have its own again," when our legislation upon cults, like our legislation upon schools, is adjusted to suit the requirements of the "spiritual order" which " is superior to the secular " (*Cath. World*, p. 583), what will be the rights and duties of citizens in non-conformity? *These:*

" We understand by religious liberty *the freedom and independence of the Church as an organic body.*"

See now how blessed a thing is a definition! Councils and prelates beyond the ocean have screamed themselves hoarse these hundreds of years past, in decrying the pernicious modern fantasy of religious liberty. Even the most solemn of late utterances of the Roman oracle, the same Encyclical and Catalogue of Principal Errors already quoted, sets this very *Catholic World*, unless its happy definition reconciles the declarations of its August number with the approval of the Pope upon the cover, in a deplorable attitude of schism and rebellion. For among the most pernicious of those damnable heresies we find held up to public abhorrence these:

" 15. That every man is free to embrace the religion he shall believe to be true, guided by the light of reason.
" 23. That the Church has not the power of

availing herself of force, or of any direct or indirect temporal power.
" 55. That the Church must be separated from the State and the State from the Church.
" 77. That in the present day it is no longer necessary that the Catholic religion shall be held as the only religion of the State, to the exclusion of all other modes of worship.
" 79. That it is false that the civil liberty of every mode of worship, and the full power given to all of overtly and publicly displaying their opinions and thoughts, conduce more easily to corrupt the morals and minds of the people and to the propagation of the evil of indifference."

But the Church in America, as we are daily assured, is a Church of progress, not of dead conservatism; of republicanism, not of autocracy; of enlightenment and free schools, not of middle-age darkness. In spite then of trans-Atlantic formulas and precedents, it could not but be the advocate of religious liberty. How noble was the conception which enabled it to maintain before the American people their favorite principle rejected by the European Church, and yet maintain that unity of doctrine, the loss of which is schism, and all by a definition! How eagerly would the fiercest ultra-montane welcome religious liberty, thus defined, to France! How gladly would the whole Spanish clergy, to-day, which for a year past has protested with all the power of its lungs and with the added force of muskets against the admission of religious liberty under one conception, accept it in the American-Catholic sense! Nay, even in those sadly diminished provinces which own the sway of the Head of the Church alone; whose governors are bishops, and whose ministers of state are cardinals; where the Jew slinks timorously into the Ghetto at night-fall lest the *sbirri* be upon him; where the American may pray to his unknown God with his countrymen under the shelter of his country's flag, but not otherwise, and the catacombs themselves no longer furnish a secure retreat for dissenting worshippers; where else than here has true religious liberty " the freedom and independence of the Church as an organic body," its highest and completest development?

They err, then (and this is part of our lesson from *The Catholic World*), who tell us that the Church is an uncertain and ductile thing, one thing in Naples and another in New York, different in the times of Hildebrand and Pius IX.; or who pretend that religious liberty is a Protestant thing, or a new thing. The Church in America to-day is as the Church in Rome in the sixteenth century; its accidents only are changed. It does not accommodate its ancient ideas to modern formulas; it takes modern formulas and fits them (by a definition) to its venerable ideas. "Religious liberty," as the American Church now professes it, is the oldest of Catholic principles. Religious liberty, as thus defined, burned Savonarola in Florence and Huss at Constance. It was to vindicate "the freedom and independence of the Church as an organic body," that the Church maintained its Inquisition in Spain, and decreed the extirpation of the Albigenses in Languedoc. In France this religious liberty, temporarily depressed by the Toleration Edict of Nantes, lifted its head awhile upon the revocation of that tyrannical measure, only to be utterly swept away in the flood of equality which has overspread that land since the Revolution. Let us hope that among us this great American principle, to which we are all devoted, may be satisfied when it drives home at sunset all the Hebrew brokers in Wall-street; when Dr. Morgan Dix begs a flag from the Prussian Consulate to protect the matins and vespers at Trinity; and when the Session Laws are regularly sent down by the Governor, instead of only occasionally by the committees, as now, for the approval or rejection of the Archbishop of New York; for then shall we approach nearer than now to the entire "freedom and independence of the Church as an organic body."

But the advanced and American Catholicism which governs the Congregation of St. Paul and *The Catholic World*, this liberalism which is abreast of the times, and seeks to make its religion the religion of the future as well as of the past, leaves us in no uncertainty what shall be in that happy day the fate of heretical creeds; when "real religious liberty," as thus defined, "the only solid basis of civil liberty," is effectively maintained. The *World* has already limited the duty of the State to the protection of those religions only "not *contra bonos mores.*" The quotations we have but just made indicate how "detrimental to morals," in the Catholic view, the Protestant systems are. This, of course, excludes them from the toleration they might otherwise claim; but their exclusion is nailed and clinched by the avowal that what Protestants "*call* their religion is a perpetual protest against what we call religion," is no religion at all therefore. Upon the whole, then, we can discern in these latest utterances of progressive Catholicism little ground for the complacency with which many Protestants are in the habit of regarding the political supremacy of that Church. Perhaps it might be worth their while to consider whether there be not color for the suggestion we have sometimes heard, that the American ecclesiastic of to-day, by virtue of the very unestablished character of his Church, of its exemption from State control and responsibility to the State, however lavishly subsidized by the State, is an ultra-montane of a new and singularly exaggerated type. Kings and emperors elsewhere, by their arbitrary interference, have succeeded in modifying that implicit devotion to the foreign domination of a Pope which after all is the highest badge of Catholicity. There is no such disturbing influence here; and what may be the full blossom and ripe fruit of this new and unpruned growth may be a curious question now, and a practical one very soon.

We come now to the last, in the disorder in which we have brought them together, but by no means the least in consequence, of the principal conclusions we find in the adverse criticisms upon the July writer. Not only is the Roman Church not formally "established" in this country, but it protests, with all the solemnity that surrounds the throne of a bishop and the press of the Catholic Publication Society, that it never, under any circumstances, can be cajoled by the entreaties of a fond and devoted State into becoming established. "Catholics have no notion," says Bishop McQuaid, "of their Church ever becoming 'the established Church,' and they are just as certain that no other Church shall ever assume to be 'the established Church' in these United States." "No Church," says *The Catholic World*, "can be the established Church here or elsewhere, unless it concedes the supremacy of the State, and consents to be its slave. This the Catholic Church can never do. . . In this country . . the civil authority has recognized . . its obligation to protect the adherents of each [religion] in the free and full enjoyment of their entire religious liberty. The State guarantees, thus, *all the freedom and protection* the Church has ever secured elsewhere by concordats. She *much prefers* freedom to slavery, and her full liberty, though shared with hostile sects, to the gilded bondage of a State Church. She neither is the Established Church, *nor can she consent to become so.*"

We leave the Bishop and the Magazine to distinguish, by the help of another definition, if they will, the doctrines we have quoted from the damnable heresies Numbers 15, 55, 77, and 79, quoted above from the Syllabus. We do not assume to judge another man's servants; to their own hierarchical Master they must stand or fall. If indeed we were reviewing the *World* as carping critics, we might Socratically ask it why the Catholic Church has not heretofore, where its word was law, enforced the preference just expressed, shattered the "gilded bondage" which we are told it abhors, and "shared with hostile sects" the "full liberty" which is so congenial and so sweet? Is it despite the choice of the Church, that it is maintained to-day as the governmental Church, with all the burdens and responsibilities which that position entails, in so many European countries?

Have our ears deceived us, and are the churchly protests with which the welkin has been ringing these few years past from Naples, and Austria, and Spain, protests against the establishment of the Church, and not, as we have been supposing, against the rude severance of some of the "gilded" chains that sustained it in its detested elevation? And why, we might ask if we were controverting the *World*, does not the Church at the Holy See itself, where it is understood to be not without influence upon legislation, accomplish that beneficent order which it so much prefers, and extend to rival religions a participation in the freedom of worship which seems to be now the exclusive privilege of the Establishment? We can anticipate the answer such questions would incur. The Church in Europe is ready enough for religious liberty, if it only knew, as well as the Church in America does, what religious liberty is, but as it supposes it to mean that the Church is to have only an equal chance with the sects, it must perforce oppose it. The Church in Europe would not cling so to establishment, if it only knew, as the American Church has learned, how all the profits of establishment are to be had without its inconveniences. And when our Unestablished Church here in New York, having secured from the State the annual donation of ten times the half million or more the State bestowed upon it in 1869, and having annihilated the State's secular education, and thus recovered here what it has lost in every Catholic country in Europe, has given actual demonstration of the advantages there are in non-establishment, then we may expect to see the Spanish clergy shouldering muskets for religious liberty instead of against it; the Neapolitan clergy disbanding their banditti and signing petitions to Parliament for disestablishment; and the Holy Father himself detaching one circlet from his triple crown, and begging the Roman Senator and Council to regard him only as the first of their clerical subjects.

The Church, then, can "do better;" so much better, in fact, that *The Catholic World* hardly speaks too strongly in saying it is "insulted" by being called the State-Church. Let us not be above learning from its bitterest enemies *why* it is in this country at least as good as established. Against the passage of the Bill for the Disestablishment of the Protestant Church in Ireland, fifty-three peers protested, "Because it is impossible to place a Church, disestablished and disendowed, and bound together only by the tie of a voluntary association, on a footing of equality with the perfect organization of the Church of Rome, whereby the laity are made completely subservient to the priesthood, the priests to the bishops, and the bishops themselves are subject to the uncontrolled authority of a foreign potentate." Before this utterance of the peers, however, that shrewd disputant, Mr. Disraeli, had said the same thing more sharply in the Commons. The only way, said he, to prevent ecclesiastical inequality in Ireland is to refuse to disestablish the Protestant Church there. For the Roman Catholic Church is already established there "as fully and completely as any power, human or divine, can be established. . . . The discipline, order, and government of the Roman Catholic Church are not voluntary. They are the creation of the simple will of a sovereign pontiff, and do not depend at all on the voluntary principle. . . I maintain, that as long as His Holiness the Pope possesses Rome, *the Roman Catholic religion, in whatever country it is found, is an Establishment.*"

Beati pacificatores! It is pleasant to reconcile adversaries. If Bishop Mc Quaid and *The Catholic World* are right, perhaps Disraeli and Derby may not be far wrong. And while the meddlesome July writer seems to have erred by his public comments on the progress the Church has made in the favor of legislators, perhaps his announcements are bad only for prematurity. Perhaps his action is like that of one who, when cunning architects and sculptors have been for years bringing to perfection the façade of a gorgeous cathedral, encumbered with scaffolds and hidden by canvas, furtively, before the last blows are struck and the last bas-reliefs set, detaching the screens that conceal it, throws untimely to view the unfinished work and the enraged artists, amid grimy machinery and smutty workmen, the rollers of logs and the pullers of wires.

.

www.ingramcontent.com/pod-product-compliance
Lightning Source LLC
Chambersburg PA
CBHW021548270326
41930CB00008B/1413

* 9 7 8 3 7 4 2 8 1 2 2 2 3 *